SHERMAN CYMRU

A Shared Experience & Sherman Cymru production

SPEECHLESS

by Linda Brogan & Polly Teale

Based on *The Silent Twins* by **Marjorie Wallace**

The Company

Natasha Gordon	Jennifer Gibbons
Demi Oyediran	June Gibbons
Emma Handy	Psychiatrist / Headmistress / Cathy
Anita Reynolds	Gloria Gibbons
Alex Waldmann	Kennedy

Director	**Polly Teale**
Designer	**Naomi Dawson**
Movement Director	**Liz Ranken**
Lighting Designer	**Chris Davey**
Sound Designer	**Peter Salem**
Assistant Sound Designer	**Keith Clouston**
Assistant Director	**Aled Pedrick**
Casting	**Amy Ball**
Voice	**Jan Haydn Rowles**

Production Managers	**Nick Allsop** & **Alison Ritchie**
Company Stage Manager	**Brenda Knight**
Deputy Stage Manager	**Clare Loxley**
Assistant Stage Manager	**Charlotte Neville**
Wardrobe Manager	**Deryn Tudor**
Production Technicians	**Gareth Evans**, **Gareth Gordon**, **Rachel Mortimer**, **Katy Stephenson**

Everything you hear solely as a voiceover
was written by the twins.

The performance will last approximately 1hrs 30 mins.

Welcome Home

by Yasmin Alibhai Brown

The story of the silent twins is in many ways a fable, a Biblical parable of the momentous post-war encounter between Caribbean and white Britons, the faithful travellers and faithless hosts. The former believed they would find a place in the ample lap of the Imperial Motherland, who had so long promised, had *promised* them her protection and much more if they were good. And they, her subjects, were very good, too good perhaps like Mr and Mrs Gibbons, parents of June and Jennifer, of whom more later.

In June 1948 the Empire Windrush sailed into Tilbury bringing the first 492 skilled migrants from Jamaica, their eyes alight with hope, ready to work hard, wearing thier best and smiling excitedly. Some sang gospels as they docked. The London Evening Standard had a front page headline: 'Welcome Home'. More ships followed from Trinidad, Barbados, other Caribbean islands and Guyana. Jobs and accommodation then were easily found but like the winter they had not yet experienced, the migrants didn't realise what was to come. They found out fast enough. Most were too polite to say so aloud, but two thirds of the natives did not want 'primitive, jungle heathens' on the streets, in pubs, clubs, workplaces or localities. A. G Bennett, a Jamaican poet and journalist wryly observed the covert racism in his novel, *Because They Know Not* (1959, Phoenix): *'Since I came 'ere I never met a single English person who 'ad any colour prejudice. Once I walked the whole length of a street looking for a room and everyone told me that he or she 'ad no prejudice against coloured people. It was the neighbour who was stupid. If we could find the 'neighbour' we could solve the entire problem. But to find 'im is the trouble! Neighbours are the worst people to live beside in this country'.*

Meanwhile, members of parliament raising their own eloquent objections gave voice and credence to the institutional hypocrisy underpinning 'coloured immigration'. With audacious plans in place to build an entire welfare state, the nation needed good, cheap, overseas workers. Didn't mean the people wanted them, or had any obligation to restrain racist contempt and worse. And worse, they still felt the country was superhumanly tolerant, and the complaining incomers wretched ingrates. (That British tradition carries on, and vigorously. Today indispensable migrant labour from the poorest countries in the globalised world face the same antipathy.)

Unlike other groups of immigrants, Caribbeans had reasons to believe they would belong in Britain. They were good Christians, had been educated by missionaries, had imbibed British values, had volunteered to fight for queen and country, particularly in the RAF. Rejection and racism made some go into denial – they carried on behaving and dressing immaculately as if that passive perseverance would, one day, bring its rewards. Some went about with their heads held high, smiles and fake pride hiding hurt. Others disengaged, set up their own shebeens or drank at home with old compatriots, spoke patois to each other, gave up on hopes of integration. For a minority disillusionment led to anger which was either internalised – leading to mental chaos – or externalised, acted out in crimes and acts of destruction. In the Gibbons family, you witness the range from denial to destruction. The father, mother and children incarnate the different reactions, as characters do on stage in the great tragedies.

Just take the scene when, in 1977, the twins get bullied and beaten in school. They get the blame; they are moved to a 'special' school. Mrs Gibbons (not up to the challenge of mothering these complicated girls) first presents to the Head the respectability of her RAF husband and churchgoing family and only towards the end, when there is nothing to lose, brings up the racial isolation her 'twinnies' must have been experiencing in an intimidating, all-white school. Later when dressing the cuts and bruises, Gloria Gibbons warns the girls not to tell their dad what happened, not to bother him.

Aubrey Gibbons emigrated in 1960, more than a decade after Windrush. By that time, he must have believed, familiarity would have seen off initial nativist hostility and things were bound to have got better, particularly as the country was freeing itself from old social constraints and the old order. Not so. The counter-culture did not naturally include black and Asian immigrants. Sure, the flower power folk just loved Motown, Ravi Shankar and Maharishi Mahesh Yogi, and mixed couples danced sometimes and there were furtive fumblings in bedrooms. Many white women went for black guys – as was beautifully captured in Andrea Levy's *Small Island*. But throughout the Sixties notices forbidding entry to 'coloured' people were commonly pasted on windows of homes and workplaces, some clubs and pubs too.

If he was confused by the contradictions Aubrey Gibbons never showed it. The son of a carpenter, he was a scholarship boy at 'an expensive school meticulously modelled on the best English examples' writes Marjorie Wallace in her book on the twins. Trained to be the perfect Edwardian English gentleman, he was polite, distant, discomfited by demonstrative, emotive behaviour. The kids were left to be managed by his wife who knew her place. Though racism must have affected his prospects, he was accepted by his peers. The twins felt no sense of place and withdrew into themselves. Experts brought in to deal with them – some well intentioned, others cruelly indifferent – focussed on inadequate parenting and the dynamics of twinning but hardly any of them considered endemic racial prejudice, the toxic milieu.

There are some telling synchronicities that show up as these two lives unravel. On the 11th of April 1981 (the birthday of the twins) the Brixton riots exploded. Black people had had enough under Thatcherism – they were no longer going to be good. Through that summer more such unrest was seen in British cities and the police acted with, by then, practised brutality. 1981 was when June and Jennifer Gibbons began their spate of drugs, crimes and wounding sexual promiscuity which they saw as self sacrifice. There was method in their madness, had been all along. Theirs, arguably, is a potted black history of those times. Mental illness among British Caribbeans – higher than the national average – in part, arises out of that bad history.

Then there is the Royal family – still loved by most ex-colonials, who are the fairy tale, the dreamy escape from the sea of disappointment and hurt. In 1977, June and Jennifer act out the Golden Jubilee in great detail, using their dolls and broadcast voices. In July 1981, the summer when the streets had burned, Diana married Charles. Gloria was glued to the TV, watching the beautiful princess and golden carriage while her daughters were breaking the law and themselves, bit by bit. It is unbearable, the juxtaposition of the white dress on a virgin going to her fate and the black girls, drunk, high, wearing strange Afro wigs and asking to be raped.

Though mute for years, theirs was not only a story of private grief and catastrophic co-dependency. Their personal tragedy flashes a blinding light on the political and social landscape of the time and of post-war migration. We need to have bifocal vision both to see and understand what happened to the babies who arrived on a propitious spring day in 1963.

"Please God, let me be bold enough to speak openly. Don't let this disease paralyse me, destroying my abilities, tying up my tongue. Like Firewood"

Jennifer

"All through my schooldays I got a strange feeling I was a boy. It's as though I'd been a boy first in my life. It wasn't anything like masturbation. But it had to be done in secret. I would get my mum's Littlewoods catalogue. I was filled with anger, rage and jealousy that a man would actually get turned on by women in the nude, and an intense hate for those models; those senseless, feminine, defenceless women.

I felt they were letting their sex down. I hated my soul for being one. I was so mad to think I had the savagely sex-mad mind of a boy, yet I had the body of a girl. The humiliation I would have to suffer as a female. All this because of Eve and that forbidden fruit. Women were to be degraded for all their life through."

June

*"Once there was 2 parrots who were brought up to live in a zoo.
Every day people would come to the zoo and see the parrots.
Sometimes the parrots would mock the talking people
and sometimes they would have a conversation between
themselves. The parrots often talked how they longed
to get back to their native land.*

*Sometimes they would ask the watchers to open the cage
door and let them out. The people would laugh and think the
parrots were kidding. Some of the children who were watching
asked their parents if they could take the parrots home.*

*Before the parents had time to answer one parrot would say:
'We're not for sale'. And the other parrot would say the same."*

Jennifer

Alex Waldmann, Demi Oyediran, Emma Handy, Anita Reynolds & Natasha Gordon

"I hate the life I am leading now. But why do I say leading? For I do not lead my life at all. It is pulled along by an invisible string. By whom? By what? A circumstance of the past. A force. I am just an onlooker."

June

"Families are so tragic, full of moments of disaster. Sometimes it's about love, mostly about hate. So that's why I could see the pretence, the pretence of a jigsaw family trying to think they fit into each other: that they've got all the right pieces."

June

Alex Waldmann, Emma Handy, Demi Oyediran, Natasha Gordon & Anita Reynolds

Dancing in Words

Excerpt from an article by Marjorie Wallace in the Sunday Times magazine, 3rd July 1994

At first June and Jennifer seemed happy, outgoing toddlers, but when they were just under four they began to ignore their parents, taking what appeared to be vows of silence and turning their backs on the outside world. They would communicate only with each other. It was not until the twins were 14 that the fact that no teacher or fellow pupil had heard them speak to an adult became a matter of concern. They were transferred to a special school, but all efforts made to prise the girls apart failed. Clamped together like limpets, they were diagnosed as 'elective mutes'.

I became involved with the twins while they were on remand awaiting trial following a spree of petty theft and arson. I was alerted to their plight by their educational psychologist, Tim Thomas, and Aubrey, their father, who showed me some of the poems, stories, and they had written while shutting themselves in their bedroom. I found their writings sensitive and moving. What fascinated me was the intensity of their imagination and the sheer efforts they had made to educate themselves.

I joined Aubrey on a visit to Pucklechurch remand centre where they were awaiting trial. The twins, now 18, were brought in, eyes downcast, propped like wooden planks against the warders. My challenge was to find the key to wind these mechanical dolls into life. I did not see them as case histories or teenage criminals. In their writings I had found shafts of wit, tenderness and lyricism kept secret so long.

Natasha Gordon & Demi Oyediran

The breakthrough came on that first visit. We were sitting facing one another watched closely by warders. When I commented on their writing talent it was like someone sitting at the bedside of comatose victims of an accident. I was rewarded with a flicker of a smile and June stuttered: 'Did you like the story? How should it end?' It gradually became clear that they thought I could be a voice for them and on each of my next visits they slipped over the exercise books in which they wrote their diaries.

June and Jennifer, physically rigid, did all their dancing in words. They communicated through thousands of them in minuscule handwriting, stitched four seams to a line. They recorded in startling images their daily anguish, the fierce psychological warfare that they inflicted on each other. Each breath one took would irritate the other; every movement one made could be the trigger for another battle. They starved and binged in turn, one forcing the other to eat two meals while she starved; then the roles would reverse. If one twin broke the elaborate rules, all the artillery they had accumulated to combat the outside world was ranged against the other.

It is through deciphering these diaries, more than a million words of them, that I grew to know the inner torment of their thoughts and began to understand how a relationship that started with something as innocent as a nursery pact could eventually become one of despair and mutual bondage.

Since no unit or secure hospital would accept these strange silent girls, they were sent to Broadmoor Special Hospital. It was a terrible and unjust sentence which deprived them of eleven years of their young womanhood. Throughout those years they continued to write diaries which they gave to me and encouraged my efforts to write their story in a book and BBC drama.

Day in and day out they dreamed of their release but when their transfer to a unit in Wales became a possibility, their old battles for their birthright re-surfaced. They decided, in order to be truly liberated into the outside world, one twin would have to sacrifice her life for the other.

Nine days before their release, when I visited them, Jennifer told me: *'I am going to die…'. 'Don't be silly,'* I replied, *'You are so young. There is no reason.' 'I just know,'* she replied, *'I just know.'*

On March 9, minutes after the twins had climbed into a minibus taking them out of Broadmoor for the last time, Jennifer slumped on her sister's shoulder. By 6.15pm that night she was dead.

The verdict at Jennifer's inquest was accidental death. The pathology reports showed that she died from an inflammation of the heart muscle that can be triggered by a host of causes.

June's reaction was one of deep grief and mourning, mixed with anger and relief. When I visited June a few days after Jennifer's death, she said, *'in some ways it was a sweet release... we were war weary. It had been a long battle. Someone had to break the vicious circle.'* She asked me if I could float a banner across the skies of Haverfordwest. *'What would it say?'* I asked. *'June is alive and well and has at last come into her own'*.

Theirs is a strange story, with an even stranger ending. The price of June's freedom appears to have been Jennifer's death, and June is now left to live for both of them. She is an attractive, maturing woman with flashes of humour, perception and insight. She keeps her life private. It is a tribute to her strong spirit that she has remained intact, not only from her years in Broadmoor, but from a lifetime's battle with the knowledge that someone else identical, but profoundly different, was sharing her soul. It is thanks to the brilliance of the twins and the courage of their family in allowing their story to be told that we have been given such unique insights into the universal dilemma where two human beings become so closely entwined that they can neither live together nor apart.

"I blame the daffodils. Who wants to hear summery sounds while they're in prison? Who wants to hear summery sounds even when they're free. Not me. I hate summer. The same old outings, happy people going on long-planned holidays. Children sucking ice-cream, pregnant women wearing blousey dresses. Why can't it be winter the whole year round. Do we really need summer?"

June

Demi Oyediran & Natasha Gordon

A Promised Land

by Polly Teale

Nearly twenty years ago I watched a documentary about the twins and was, like so many others, fascinated by the story. That two young women so full of hope, aspiration and imagination could end up in Broadmoor for committing violent crimes seemed like a modern tragedy.

It was Linda, my co-writer, who realised that the summer the twins were convicted of arson was the same summer that the race riots were happening all over Britain, and also the summer that Prince Charles married Lady Diana. It became clear that the twins' experience was part of a bigger story: the story of Imperialism and its legacy. Aubrey, the twins' father, was a scholarship boy at a school in the West Indies that was modelled on an English public school. The pupils grew up learning the kings and queens of England. To come to the Mother Country and join the RAF was a lifelong ambition. Growing up in a colony England was seen as a promised land. When he arrived in Britain with his young family he thought that he was coming home. But for all his efforts to belong he remained isolated within the RAF, unable to assimilate into this most British of institutions. His wife Gloria struggled to fit in with the RAF wives, arranging tupperware parties and coffee mornings to little avail.

Our story begins when the twins are fourteen and are being bullied at school and returning home to enact the Queen's Silver Jubilee in their bedroom. Linda and I wanted to investigate the complexity of being placed in thrall to a system that ultimately alienated and rejected them.

The twins' struggle to find a language in a hostile world reminds us all of our human need to be heard and the dramatic consequences if we are denied that right.

> *"First of all let's get one thing straight: nobody knows us really. All these things you say about us are wrong."*
>
> June

Company

Left vertical line (rear to front): Gareth Evans, Nancy Meckler, Hanna Osmolska, Aled Pedrick, Peter Salem, Alice Baynham, Kenon Man, Demi Oyediran.
Centre: Clare Loxley, Chris Davey, Kate Perridge, Liz Ranken, Linda Brogan, Emma Handy.
Right: Nick Allsop, Charlotte Neville, Amy Hodge, Polly Teale, Alex Waldmann, Natasha Gordon, Anita Reynolds, Naomi Dawson

Natasha Gordon

Jennifer Gibbons

Trained: Guildhall School of Music and Drama.

Theatre includes: *Mules, The Exception and the Rule* (Young Vic); *As You Like It, Cymbeline, The Tamer Tamed* (RSC); *Inside Out* (Clean Break Theatre Company); *Aladdin* (Lyric Hammersmith/Told by an Idiot); *Clubland* (Royal Court); *Top Girls* (BAC); *Arabian Nights* (Young Vic Tour).

Television includes: *Law and Order, The Bill* (ITV); *10 Days to War, Little Miss Jocelyn, Doctors, Holby City* (BBC).

Demi Oyediran

June Gibbons

Theatre includes: *Joe Turner's Come and Gone* (Young Vic); *Twelfth Night, Here Lies Mary Splindler* (RSC); *Death and the King's Horseman* (National Theatre); *Fairtrade* (Pleasance); *Twelfth Night* (The Orange Tree Theatre); *Oxford Street* (Royal Court); *Graceland* (24hrs Plays, Old Vic); *Bullet Proof Soul* (Birmingham Rep).

TV includes: *Consuming Passion* (BBC4); *W10 LDN* (Kudos).

Film includes: *Apples and Oranges* (CH4/IWC Media).

Emma Handy

Psychiatrist / Headmistress / Cathy

Trained: LAMDA.

Theatre includes: *Edward Gants Amazing Feats of Loneliness* (Headlong); *Crown Matrimonial* (ACT); *A Midsummer Nights Dream* (Lisbon International Opera festival); *Vincent in Brixton* (National Theatre/West End); *50 Revolutions* (Trafalgar Studios); *Merchant of Venice, Bad Weather, Twelfth Night* (RSC); *The Wood Demon* (West End); *Csongor es Tunde* (Merlin International Theatre, Budapest).

TV includes: *Wire in the Blood (Series 2, 3, 4, 5, 6), Silent Witness, Beneath The Skin, William & Mary (Series 2), Hear the Silence, Doctors, The Bill, Real Crime, Emma Brody, See Me, Innocents – Bristol Babies, Black Cab, Pretending To Be Judith.*

Film includes: *Balham vs Clapham, Vincent in Brixton, Vacuums, Iris, Club Le Monde, Velvet Goldmine.*

Polly Teale (Co-writer, *Speechless*)

Anita Reynolds

Gloria Gibbons

Trained: Royal Welsh College of Music and Drama.

Theatre includes: Theatr Iolo, Hijinx, Theatre Centre, London Bubble, Nottingham Playhouse and Sherman Theatre Company.

TV includes: *Being Human, Casualty, The Bench* (BBC); *Belonging* (BBC Wales); *Dau Dy a Ni* (ITV Wales); *Caerdydd, Gwaith Cartref* (Fiction Factory).

Film includes: *Paradise Grove* (Charlie Harris); *Colonial Gods* (Iris Prize); *Summertime* (Tornado Films).

Alex Waldmann

Kennedy

Trained: LAMDA.

Theatre includes: *Rope* (Almeida Theatre); *Shraddha* (Soho Theatre); *Hamlet, Twelfth Night* (Donmar West End); *Troilus and Cressida* (Cheek by Jowl); *Angry Young Man* (Trafalgar Studios/Pleasance Edinburgh); *Hobson's Choice* (Chichester Festival); *Waltz of the Toreadors* (Chichester Minerva); *Macbeth* (West Yorkshire Playhouse); *Big Love* (Gate Theatre); *Romeo and Juliet* (Birmingham Rep); *Hortensia and the Museum of Dreams* (Finborough Theatre); *Fishbowl* (Theatre503).

TV includes: *Psychoville, First Light* (BBC)

Alex's production company SEArED is co-producing *Pedestrian* alongside Bristol Old Vic and Theatre Bristol at Underbelly during the Fringe Festival.

Creative Team

Linda Brogan (Co-writer, *Speechless*)

Polly Teale

Director and Co-writer (*Speechless*)

Polly is Joint Artistic Director of Shared Experience.

For Shared Experience: *The Glass Menagerie*, *Mine* (written and directed), *Ten Tiny Toes*, *Kindertransport*, *Jane Eyre* (adapted and directed), *Brontë*, *After Mrs Rochester* (written and directed – Best Director, Evening Standard Awards; Best West End Production, Time Out Awards), *Madame Bovary*, *The Clearing*, *A Doll's House*, *The House of Bernarda Alba*, *Desire Under the Elms*.

Co-directed with Nancy Meckler: *War and Peace* and *Mill on the Floss*.

Other theatre includes: *Angels and Saints* (Soho Theatre); *The Glass Menagerie* (Lyceum, Edinburgh); *Miss Julie* (Young Vic); *Babies, Uganda, Catch* (Royal Court); *A Taste of Honey* (ETT); *Somewhere* (National Theatre); *Waiting at the Waters Edge* (Bush Theatre); *What Is Seized* (Drill Hall).

Linda Brogan

Co-writer (*Speechless*)

Linda's writing credits include *Basil and Beattie*, produced at the Royal Exchange and Liverpool Everyman, which won the NWP 21st anniversary commission; *What's in the Cat*, produced by Contact and Royal Court, nominated for MEN Best New Play, published by Methuen; *Black Crows*, produced by Clean Break at The Arcola and shortlisted for The Alfred Fagon Award and The Susan Smith BlackBurn Prize, and published by Oberon.

Marjorie Wallace (Author, *The Silent Twins*)

Marjorie Wallace, CBE

Author (*The Silent Twins*)

Marjorie Wallace CBE is an award-winning investigative journalist, author and broadcaster and is Chief Executive of SANE, the leading mental health charity she founded following her series of articles in The Times, '*The Forgotten Illness*'.

After graduating in psychology and philosophy from London University, she worked on the *Frost Programme* and later as reporter and director for the BBC's *Current Affairs* programmes. In 1972 she joined the Sunday Times 'Insight Team', exposing the Thalidomide tragedy, and was co-author of the book *Suffer the Children*. She also wrote the book and screenplay for the Emmy winning drama, *On Giant's Shoulders* – the story of a family who adopted a Thalidomide child. Marjorie has received numerous awards for her journalism and books including Campaigning Journalist of the Year on two occasions.

Her book *The Silent Twins* became a best seller and the film made from her screenplay was voted best docudrama in the USA (1988). She later wrote and presented provocative television documentaries – *Whose Mind is it Anyway?* and *Circles of Madness* – and gained a reputation as an international lecturer and broadcaster.

She is an Honorary Fellow of the Royal College of Psychiatrists; Doctor of Science (City University) and a Fellow of University College,

London. She has been cited in the Daily Mail and many other publications as among Britain's most influential women and in 2008 was selected as one of the 60 most influential people in shaping the history of the National Health Service.

Marjorie Wallace married psychoanalyst Count Andrzej Skarbek, with whom she had three sons. She now lives in North London with the founder of New Scientist and London Weekend Television, Tom Margerison, and their daughter.

Naomi Dawson

Designer

Trained: Wimbledon School of Art and Kunstacademie, Maastricht.

Designs include: *The Glass Menagerie* (Shared Experience); *Amgen: Broken* (Sherman Cymru); *The Typist* (Sky Arts); *The Gods Weep* (RSC); *Krieg Der Bilder* (Staatstheater Mainz); *Rutherford and Son* (Northern Stage); *Three More Sleepless Nights* (Lyttelton, National Theatre); *The Container* (Young Vic); *King Pelican, Speed Death of the Radiant Child* (Drum Theatre, Plymouth); *If That's All There Is* (Lyric); *State of Emergency, Mariana Pineda* (Gate); *…Sisters* (Gate/Headlong); *Can any Mother Help Me?* (Foursight, UK Tour); *Stallerhof, Richard III, The Cherry Orchard, Summer Begins* (Southwark Playhouse); *Phaedra's Love* (Barbican Pit and Bristol Old Vic); *Different Perspectives* (Contact Theatre); *The Pope's Wedding, Forest of Thorns* (Young Vic Studio); *Market Tales* (Unicorn); *Attempts on Her Life, Widows, Touched* (BAC); *In Blood, Venezuela, Mud, Trash, Headstone* (Arcola); *A Thought in Three Parts* (Burton Taylor, Oxford).

Film credits include: Costume design for short film *Love After a Fashion*, Set design for *Fragile* by Idris Khan.

Naomi is part of artists collective SpRoUt recently exhibiting in Galerija SC, Zagreb.

Chris Davey

Lighting Designer

For Shared Experience: *The Caucasian Chalk Circle, Jane Eyre, Brontë, Madame Bovary, After Mrs Rochester, A Passage to India, Mill on the Floss, Anna Karenina, The Tempest, Desire Under the Elms, The Danube, War and Peace* (co-production with the National Theatre).

Chris has designed extensively for the National Theatre, RSC, Shared Experience Theatre, Royal Court, Hampstead Theatre, Lyric Hammersmith, Royal Exchange Manchester, West Yorkshire Playhouse, Royal Lyceum Edinburgh and Birmingham Rep.

Recent designs include: *Death of a Salesman* (West Yorkshire Playhouse); *Morecambe* (Duchess Theatre); *Carlos Acosta and Guests* (London Coliseum); *The Pianist, Everyone Loves a Winner, Carlos Acosta* (Manchester International Festival); *The Last Witch* (Edinburgh International Festival/Traverse); *Pornography* (Traverse Edinburgh, Birmingham Rep); Matthew Bourne's *The Car Man* (Sadler's Wells/Old Vic and international tour); *Peer Gynt* (National Theatre of Scotland).

Opera includes: *Romeo et Juliette* (Opera Ireland); *Hippolyte et Aricie* (Nationale Reisopera Netherlands); *L'Arbore di Diana* Valencia, *I Capuleti E I Montecchi* (Opera North, Melbourne, Sydney Opera House); *Skellig* (The Sage Gateshead); *Aida Houston, Bird of Night* (Royal Opera House); *Bluebeard* Bregenz, *Jephtha* (English National Opera/Welsh National Opera, Copenhagen); *The Magic Flute* (Welsh National Opera); Eight seasons for Grange Park Opera; *The Rake's Progress, The Turn of the Screw* (Aldeburgh Festival); *The Picture of Dorian Gray* (Monte Carlo).

Peter Salem

Sound Designer

Peter Salem's sound scores have become a major ingredient in Shared Experience's work: *The Glass Menagerie, Mine, Ten Tiny Toes, War & Peace, Kindertransport, Orestes, Brontë, A Passage to India, The Clearing, Mill on the Floss, The House of Bernarda Alba, Jane Eyre, The Tempest, Anna Karenina.*

Other theatre credits include: *The Crucible, The Miser,* Robert Lépage's *A Midsummer Night's Dream* (all at the National Theatre); *Julius Caesar, Murder in the Cathedral* (RSC); and work for the Royal Court, Traverse, Lyric Hammersmith and Nottingham Playhouse.

Peter's contemporary dance scores have been performed by Second Stride and Zaragosa Ballet Company.

Film and TV – many dramas and documentaries, including: *5 Daughters* (a three-part drama recently broadcast on BBC1); *Great Expectations, The Other Boleyn Girl, Sex, the City and Me, Beau Brummell* (BBC); *Falling, Trial and Retribution, Thursday the 12th, Alive and Kicking* (Cinema/C4); *The Vice, Painted Lady* (ITV); *Francesco's Venice, Simon Schama's The Power of Art: Caravaggio, Thrown to the Lions, Sea of Cortez, 21Up, The Spy Who Caught a Cold, I Met Adolf Eichmann, Three Salons at the Seaside, Swimmers.*

Keith Clouston

Assistant Sound Designer

Theatre includes: As composer – *King Lear,
The Winter's Tale, Julius Caesar, Coriolanus,
Night of the Soul* (RSC); *The UN Inspector*
(National Theatre); *Coriolanus* (Old Vic); *Julius
Caesar, The Resistible Rise of Arturo Ui, The
Magic Carpet* (Lyric Hammersmith); *Baghdad
Wedding* (Soho Theatre); *The Eleventh Capital*
(Royal Court); *Tamburlaine* (Bristol Old Vic/
Barbican); *A Midsummer Night's Dream,
The Comedy of Errors, Paradise Lost, Twelfth
Night, Cyrano de Bergerac* (Bristol Old Vic);
Electra, Trojan Women (Cambridge Arts
Theatre). As musician – *The Comedy of Errors*
(RSC, Young Vic and Shakespeare's Globe);
Peer Gynt (National Theatre).

Television includes: *Later with Jools Holland,
The Girlie Show, Painted Lady, The Life
of Mohammed, Glastonbury '99, The Bill.*

Radio includes: As composer – *Baghdad
Wedding.* As musician – *The Andy Kershaw
Show, Loose Ends, Antony and Cleopatra,
The Iliad.*

Other: As composer – *Tears* (Spitalfields
Festival/Royal Academy of Music), *Songs,
Compositions & Improvisations* (ICA).
As musician – *Natacha Atlas* (Glastonbury
Festival, Queen Elizabeth's Hall, ICA,
Shepherds Bush Empire, Europe,
USA, Brazil).

Liz Ranken

Movement Director

Liz Ranken has been working with Shared
Experience for 17 years, and as Movement
Director plays a key role in rehearsals.

For Shared Experience: *The Glass Menagerie,
The Caucasian Chalk Circle, Mine, Ten Tiny
Toes, War & Peace, Kindertransport, Orestes,
Madame Bovary, A Passage to India, A Doll's
House, Jane Eyre, The House of Bernarda Alba,
The Tempest, Mill on the Floss, Anna Karenina.*

As Director and Performer: *Summat A-do-wi
Weddins* (Place Portfolio Choreographic
Award); *Theory of Love; Ooh; Funk Off Green*
(Capital Award); *Venus and Adonis* (with
Rebecca McCutcheon).

As Performer: *Terminatress* (with Rae Smith);
The Big Tease (Grassmarket Project); work
with Gloria, CAT A Company ENO. Founder
member of DV8. Winner of the 1992 Dance
Umbrella Time Out Award.

Liz is an Associate Movement Director for
the RSC and completed *The Histories* in
2007. She has also worked extensively with
Dominic Cooke including *Arabian Nights,
Fireface* and *My Mother Said I Never Should.*

TV and film include: As Performer – *Silences;
3 Steps to Heaven; Touched; Edward II;
Pet Shop Boys Tour.* As Choreographer –
Alive and Kicking.

Liz also works professionally as a commissioned
painter – see www.lizranken.com

Aled Pedrick

Assistant Director

Trained: Guildhall School of Music and Drama.

Theatre includes (as an actor): *The Nutcracker* (Theatre Royal, Bath); *Ceisio'i Bywyd Hi* (Welsh translation of *Attempts On Her Life* – Sherman Cymru); *Doctor Who* (BBC); *Gari Tryfan* (S4C); *Lewis* (ITV); *Aki Nabalu* (Astro, Malaysia).

Aled also teaches at Guildhall School of Music and Drama as a member of the voice department.

Brenda Knight

Company Stage Manager

Trained: Royal Welsh College of Music and Drama.

She has worked, enjoyably, many times with Sherman Cymru but this is a first with Shared Experience. Brenda is also a founder member of Mappa Mundi theatre company which tours the UK every year.

Clare Loxley

Deputy Stage Manager

Recent theatre includes: *Macbeth*, *Troilus & Cressida*, *Cymbeline*, *The Changeling*, *Othello*, *Homebody/Kabul* (Cheek By Jowl); *The Gigli Concert* (Druid); *Deep Cut*, *Merlin and the Cave of Dreams* (Sherman Cymru); *Life x 3*, *Matilda & Duffy* (Watermill Theatre); *Antigone*, *A Conversation*, *Cyrano de Bergerac*, *Come Blow Your Horn*, *Playboy of the Western World* (Royal Exchange, Manchester); *East* (Leicester Haymarket).

Charlotte Neville

Assistant Stage Manager

Theatre includes – As designer: *Missing, Finding Leaves for Soup* (Theatr Iolo); *The Long Way Home, The Other Woman* (Hijinx); *A Real Princess* (WNO MAX). As ASM – *The Stories of Hans Christian Andersen* (Sherman Theatre Company); *The Snow Queen* and *A Christmas Carol* (Sherman Cymru).

Charlotte has also worked with Sherman Cymru's Acting Out Cardiff group, working with students to design and produce their shows. Her work also involves tutoring Props and Puppetry at the Royal Welsh College of Music and Drama.

Shared Experience

Shared Experience is committed to creating theatre that goes beyond our everyday lives, giving form to the hidden world of emotion and imagination. We see the rehearsal process as a genuinely open forum for asking questions and taking risks that define the possibilities of performance. At the heart of the company's work is the power and excitement of the performer's physical presence and the collaboration between actor and audience – a shared experience.

Joint Artistic Directors
Nancy Meckler & **Polly Teale**
Administrative Producer **Jon Harris**
Associate Director **Kate Saxon**
Marketing Consultant **Mark Slaughter**
Assistant Producer **Hanna Osmolska**
Finance Officer **Helen Hillman**

Board of Directors
Daniel Astaire
Dame Joan Bakewell (Chair)
Diane Benjamin
Neil Brener
Olga Edridge
Jeffery Kissoon
Clare Lawrence Moody
Alan Rivett

Patrons
Anonymous, Sarah & Neil Brener,
Paula Clemett & Geoff Westmore,
Lady Hatch, Ann Orton.

Liz Ranken

Special thanks to: Dominic Cook, Ruth Little and all at the Royal Court, Wendy Lilly and the staff at Sane, Steven Butler, Tim Saunders at Alford House, Liz Holmes at ArtsAdmin, Matt Roe at Dance Base, Peter Knight.

The commissioning of the script of this play was generously co-funded by a gift from Paula Clemett and Geoff Westmore.

Photography: Ellie Kurttz
Graphic Design: Eureka!

Education

Shared Experience's Youth & Education work is central to the company.
All the productions are accompanied by an Education Programme.

Workshops

Suitable for Drama/English Literature students at: GCSE, A Level and in Higher Education. Two types of workshop are available to book:

- *Speechless* – the rehearsal process and production
- Shared Experience Process – innovative and unique exercises from the rehearsal room

To book Shared Experience workshops, please contact us on **020 7587 1596** or contact **hanna@sharedexperience.org.uk**

For further Information or to discuss options for your school, contact Associate Director, Kate Saxon on **kate@sharedexperience.org.uk**

Post-Show Discussions

Offer a chance to stay behind after a performance to meet the cast for Q & A. Contact your theatre box office to check the date.

Theatre Days and Other Events

There are various events being held at the theatres on tour, such as Theatre Days (a chance to learn more from behind the scenes from the actors and creative team), pre-performance debates and pre-show foyer performances by young people. Please contact the theatre for further information.

"Shared Experience is one of the most distinctive theatre companies in the land. Those who have seen the company are unlikely to forget its thrilling productions"

Support Shared Experience

Become a Friend or Patron of Shared Experience

We hope you enjoy watching our work onstage. It's the result of an enormous amount of careful preparation, and represents only part of what we achieve.

Our productions come about as the result of a unique creative process led by our Joint Artistic Directors, Nancy Meckler and Polly Teale. We conduct an intensive period of collaboration through script commission, development and workshops with performers. The writer works with the director and actors to evolve a visual and imaginative language for the particular piece. Our process is costly, but it's vital to assure the quality of what you see onstage.

Central to our work are the activities of the Youth & Education department under the leadership of our Associate Director, Kate Saxon. We offer schools' workshops, pre- and post-show talks with members of the company, and our trademark "Inside Out" days at which school parties gain a unique insight into the production process.

By becoming a Friend or Patron of Shared Experience you directly help us to continue our commitment to excellence both onstage and in our work with young people in schools as well as enjoying special benefits.

To discuss joining us please contact:

Jon Harris, Administrative Producer, Shared Experience
Tel: 020 7587 1596
Email: jon@sharedexperience.org.uk

www.sharedexperience.org.uk

Supported by
ARTS COUNCIL ENGLAND

SHERMAN CYMRU

We aim to make and present great theatre that is ambitious, inventive and memorable for our audiences, and to create strong, responsive and enriching relationships with our communities. We strive to create the best theatre we can; to achieve a distinct and diverse programme for our audiences; to engage our communities in the creative process of theatre making; and to make a lasting contribution to the national and international development of theatre in Wales. We produce work in both English and Welsh, and tour widely within Wales and the UK.

For more information about Sherman Cymru events visit

www.shermancymru.co.uk

Cyngor Celfyddydau Cymru
Arts Council of Wales

Deep Cut by Philip Ralph, 2008.
Photo by Farrows Creative

Llwyth (Tribe) by Dafydd James, 2010.
Photo by Farrows Creative

Sherman Cymru Redevelopment

The Sherman building has closed for a £5.4 million redevelopment and the fundraising campaign is gathering pace. We have secured £130,000 from the Welsh Assembly Government as well as support from two important trusts, Garfield Weston Foundation and the Colwinston Charitable Trust.

From the generous individual donations that our audiences and supporters have been giving, we have already raised an amazing £32,000. Thank you so much for your continued and loyal support so far but we still need your help!

You can make a difference and change the way you and thousands of people experience the Sherman in the future. Here are just two examples of ways which you can help to raise the remaining £1.3 million:

The Foyer Appeal
Give as much as you can and help transform the foyer and entrance to the theatre.

Currency Exchange Appeal
Get rid of your unwanted holiday coins and make a difference by donating your foreign currency to us. Sherman Cymru can exchange any amount and any currency and all proceeds will go directly to our Redevelopment Campaign. Large or small, Sherman Cymru accepts it all!

If you'd like to know more about the campaign please contact:
Suzanne Carter – **029 2064 6970**
suzanne@shermancymru.co.uk
www.shermancymru.co.uk/capital

Sherman Cymru Staff

One in four people experiences a mental health problem. SANE offers help to those affected, their friends and families.

SANE

Meeting the challenge of mental illness. Support and information are available throughout the day with SANE Services:

SANEline
- Telephone helpline offering specialist support and information
- Open from 6pm until 11pm, 365 days a year
- *0845 767 8000*

SANE Discussion Board
- Onilne community offering peer support, advice and information
- Access 24 hours a day
- *www.sane.org.uk/DB*

SANEmail
- Information and help available vie e-mail: *sanemail@sane.org.uk*

SANE (limited by guarantee) Registered Company Number: 2114937 Registered Charity Number: 296572

SPEECHLESS

Adapted for the stage by Linda Brogan and Polly Teale
Based on The Silent Twins *by* Marjorie Wallace

Characters

JUNE
JENNIFER
PSYCHIATRIST
HEADMISTRESS
GLORIA
CATHY
KENNEDY

Note

Speeches in italics are excerpts from the real twins' actual diaries, read in voice-over.

A forward slash (/) indicates the point at which the next speaker interrupts.

This text went to press before the end of rehearsals and so may differ slightly from the play as performed.

In the darkness we hear the voice-overs of the TWINS *each reading from their diaries.*

The voices start to overlap and grow into a cacophony of words.

Through the darkness we see the TWINS *gradually becoming visible in their prison cell. They are clinging to the frame of their bunk beds, hiding from one another.*

JUNE. *First of all, let's get one thing straight: nobody knows us really. All these things you say about us are wrong.*

JENNIFER. *What a senseless degrading havoc I have made of my poor, sweet, human life.*

JUNE. *I hate the life I am leading now. But why do I say 'leading'? For I do not lead my life at all. It is pulled along by an invisible string. By whom? By what? A circumstance of the past. A force. I am just an onlooker.*

JENNIFER. *Please God, let me be bold enough to speak openly. Don't let this disease paralyse me, destroying my abilities, tying up my tongue.*

JUNE. *And she will weep uncontrollably; only for herself as though she were watching a sad film in the movies. And she will weep for the character, only because she recognises this character to be herself.*

JENNIFER. *Useless day, there seems no reason to get up at all.*

JUNE. *Winter is here and all the birds will fly back south. I wish I could be with them.*

I blame the daffodils. Who wants to hear summery sounds while they're in prison? Who wants to hear summery sounds even when they're free. Not me. I hate summer. The same old outings, happy people going on long-planned holidays. Children sucking ice cream, pregnant women wearing blousey dresses. Why can't it be winter the whole year round? Do we really need summer?

JENNIFER. *We could not possibly have been born like that. It grew on us, as the years developed; self-consciousness, frustration, thwarted ambitions.*

JUNE. *I want to escape her. One of us is plotting to kill one of us. How will it end? We scheme, we plot and who will win?*

JENNIFER. *I feel so forsaken. I always seem to lose. June has won all the battles. Her thoughts, her words, her wicked, beautiful words make her a winner.*

JUNE. *I say to myself, how can I get rid of my own shadow? Impossible or not impossible? Without my shadow would I die? Without my shadow would I gain life?*

JENNIFER. *Where will it all end? In death? In separation? I cannot help it. She cannot help it. It sends murder into my heart and rage into my head.*

1982. Broadmoor

A prison cell with bunk beds.

The following sequence has the quality of a nightmare although it is in fact happening. The TWINS *are hiding from one another either side of their bunk beds, clinging to the bed frame. We hear their quickened breath and sense that they are both terrified. It is as if each fears they are going to be killed by the other. They edge around the perimeter of the bunk beds until finally* JENNIFER *makes a lunge for* JUNE.

The TWINS *fight.*

The sound of an alarm ringing.

It is getting slowly louder.

The fight slows down so we can see both the violence and the extreme dependency of their relationship; moments of embrace and clinging, as well as a struggle to separate, to crush and destroy, to suffocate the other.

Darkness.

Solitary

JUNE *and* JENNIFER *sit on chairs in separate cells in solitary confinement.*

Both are completely still, their faces impassive, staring at the wall opposite.

The door to JENNIFER*'s cell opens.*

A female PSYCHIATRIST *enters, carrying a clipboard with a questionnaire.*

This is a ritual they have both been through before.

PSYCHIATRIST. I'm here to tell you, Jennifer, that your time in solitary will be a maximum of four days, assuming there is no further offence. As you know, that period may be reduced if you agree to a dialogue that would help you understand and manage your behaviour. There are, as you know, a number of initiatives within Broadmoor to help inmates combat violent tendencies. They are, however, of no use unless the offender recognises their behaviour and has a desire to change it...

Pause.

Could you tell me, Jennifer, what triggered your feelings of violence towards your sister?

Silence.

Is that a feeling that you recognise?

Silence.

Is there a thought or collection of thoughts that you can identify?

Pause.

Can you remember when you first felt these feelings?

Pause.

Do they remind you of a person or situation?

Pause.

Can you describe them to me...

Very well. As you wish. If you should change your mind, I will be more than happy to help...

The PSYCHIATRIST *is getting ready to leave.*

JENNIFER *suddenly stands and snatches the* PSYCHIATRIST's *clipboard and pen.*

JUNE *stands at exactly the same moment in her separate cell.*

JENNIFER *writes on the* PSYCHIATRIST's *questionnaire.*

JENNIFER *is writing furiously.*

She stops.

JENNIFER *gives the clipboard back to the* PSYCHIATRIST.

The PSYCHIATRIST *reads the clipboard:* JUNE *speaks the words live;* JENNIFER's *words are voice-over.*

JUNE *and* JENNIFER. There was once a wild horse who lived in the woods. If people came near her she would run away. She was so fast that no one ever saw her, though they heard the sound of her hooves. The people decided the horse must be tamed. They set off into the woods with a bridle and a saddle and a whip. They searched for many days but never once saw the wild horse, though they often saw the tracks she left in the earth. Soon the people began to say that the horse had wings and that was why no one could find her.

The PSYCHIATRIST *looks up after reading the story.*

JENNIFER *and* JUNE *sit down at exactly the same time.*

Both stare at the wall as before.

The PSYCHIATRIST *bends down so she is level with* JENNIFER's *eyes, inches from her face.*

PSYCHIATRIST. Why did you stop talking to us?

The playground bell rings.

July 1977. Playground

The sound of children's voices shouting at a deafening pitch.

JUNE *and* JENNIFER *stand facing one another, with one arm cradled above their heads, like wounded birds trying to protect themselves.*

Their school blazers and bags are strewn across the playground tarmac, trampled into the dirt. Their hair and clothes are messed up.

Amidst the shouting are racist taunts and references to the TWINS' *strange speech. They are told to 'Go back to the jungle' and 'learn to speak English'. We hear the words 'wog', 'sambo', 'nignog'. Their surname, Gibbons, is used in reference to the animal, as children make monkey noises and sing 'Do the Funky Gibbon'.*

During the following scene, we can see the TWINS *in the playground, moving slowly in unison as if someone were pulling their strings. They pick up their bags and school blazers and ties and put them back on.*

The Headteacher's Office

GLORIA GIBBONS, JUNE *and* JENNIFER*'s mother, wears her best coat and hat, and carries a handbag and matching gloves.*

She is nervous but holds her head high, trying to survive this ordeal with dignity.

She has a strong West Indian accent but here talks with a clipped telephone voice.

The HEADMISTRESS *enters and stands opposite* GLORIA.

Lights up, as GLORIA *takes her gloves off and places them with her handbag on her lap.*

HEADMISTRESS. For the two weeks that constitute the rest of the summer term we've decided that June and Jennifer will stay inside during break. They will leave school ten minutes before the final bell to avoid a recurrence of recent events. Whilst we understand that the twins did not in any way provoke the attack, it is our belief that their refusal to integrate themselves with their classmates caused the hostility. I would strongly advise that they abandon this behaviour before it causes more problems of the kind we witnessed today.

GLORIA. Them always been quiet.

HEADMISTRESS. If they were unable to speak that would be different. This is a choice they're making.

GLORIA. Them always been shy.

HEADMISTRESS. They are fourteen years old; they are no longer children. They refuse to be separated; they won't eat or drink or use the lavatory. They won't make eye contact or respond in any way to teachers or pupils.

GLORIA. The twinnies is good girls.

HEADMISTRESS. There is only so much that we at the school can do if they refuse to cooperate. The Eastgate Centre has agreed to take them in the autumn.

Their special teacher will be Miss Arthur.

GLORIA. They come from a good home. A good family.

HEADMISTRESS. If she can quell their disruptive behaviour maybe they can be reintegrated at a future date.

GLORIA. Decent. Respectable. We go to church every Sunday.

HEADMISTRESS. I wasn't implying –

GLORIA. Them daddy in the Royal Air Force.

HEADMISTRESS. I didn't mean –

GLORIA. Assisitant Air Traffic Controller. Him Corporal now. Hard-working. Responsible –

HEADMISTRESS. I'm sure he is, Mrs Gibbons –

GLORIA. Never a day off in twenty-two year a service.

HEADMISTRESS. Thank you for coming today. I wish you, and the twins, all the very best.

The HEADMISTRESS *offers her hand to* GLORIA, *who realises the interview is over.*

GLORIA *shakes the* HEADMISTRESS*'s hand.*

GLORIA *gathers her handbag and gloves.*

We are aware of the TWINS *still picking up their belongings from the playground floor.*

Just as GLORIA *is about to leave, she turns back and looks at the* HEADMISTRESS.

GLORIA. Sunday me there in the front room a do the customary dust. Me go from one photo atop the glass cabinet to the next.

See them there.

Standing amongst all the other children in the class. Eleven, twelve, thirteen, them always the only coloured children in the picture. In your school. In the RAF base. On the entire estate. In the whole of this parish.

HEADMISTRESS. There's nothing we can do about that, Mrs Gibbons.

GLORIA. Me look at the photographs.

Each year it getting worse.

Them favour ghost while the other children thrive.

HEADMISTRESS. I'm sorry, Mrs Gibbons, but I'm not sure what you're trying / to say.

GLORIA. Thank you. Thank you for your time.

Lights change.

JUNE. *Families are so tragic, full of moments of disaster. Sometimes it's about love, mostly about hate. So that's why I could see the pretence, the pretence of a jigsaw family trying to think they fit into each other: that they've got all the right pieces.*

Silver Jubilee

The TWINS *are in their bedroom.*

Through their bedroom door, GLORIA *anxiously enters with ointment and cotton wool.*

GLORIA *attends* JENNIFER*'s swollen bloody lip with the ointment.*

GLORIA. We won't tell Daddy, you hear. We don't want upset him. You fall over, if him ask. No point getting him all upset. You know how him stay. Say you slip on the stairs where the carpet come loose.

GLORIA *brushes dust from their blazers, straightens their clothes, tidies their hair.*

Go wash your face. Clean yourself up. Change out a you good uniform.

GLORIA *strips each* TWIN *of their blazer and puts them over her arm.*

Me a go sponge them, mend the rip, no one will know the difference. Me make your favourite. Sausage. Chips. Crinkle-cut. Peas. Not from tin, from packet. And jam roly-poly, no custard. Eh. What you say?

GLORIA *leaves the bedroom with the blazers.*

GLORIA *pops her head back in.*

Me turn up the telly as usual to warn of *The Generation Game.*

JUNE *gets her white dolls from the cases under the bunk beds.*

The dolls are dressed in outfits the TWINS *have been making.*

JUNE *arranges the dolls into rows.*

JENNIFER *is making a parallel row of dolls.*

After watching them for a bit, GLORIA *leaves the room.*

Both TWINS *sing 'God Save the Queen' as they studiously fix their row.*

JUNE. Do it properly.

JENNIFER. I am doing it properly.

JUNE. Make sure they're straight.

JENNIFER. They are straight.

JUNE. It's not right if they're not straight.

JUNE *grabs 'Her Majesty' out of* JENNIFER*'s row of dolls.*

That's Her Majesty. That's why she's in pink.

Pass us the carriage.

JUNE *passes* JENNIFER *a tinfoil-covered shoebox.*

JENNIFER *sits the Queen inside and* JENNIFER *puts a male doll in the carriage.*

JENNIFER *pulls their home-made microphones from under the bunk beds.*

JUNE *retrieves their miniscule scripts, but immediately starts writing on them.*

We've only got ten minutes. I'm cutting the horses.

JENNIFER. My bits.

JUNE. They don't go properly. It's too messy.

JENNIFER. I won't have hardly anything to say.

JUNE. It's better to skip straight to St Paul's.

Just don't say them bits.

JUNE *hands* JENNIFER *her edited script.*

Ready. One. Two. Three.

JUNE *presses their tape recorder on.*

JENNIFER *pushes the shoebox carriage.*

JUNE *gets the dolls to wave mini Union flags.*

They commentate in RP.

The Queen's golden carriage leaves the gates of Buckingham Palace.

Through the gates of Buckingham Palace they encounter the crowd.

Cheering.

Both girls cheer as if a crowd.

They wave flags. Lines of people. Some have queued for two weeks now. Flasks. Bedding. Tents.

JENNIFER. We have a party here from RAF base Haverfordwest. Lovely to see the whole community, Mrs Miller.

JUNE (*speaking as the blonde Barbie*). Call me Marilyn. These are my daughters, June and Jennifer.

JENNIFER. This afternoon, the Royal Air Force will be flying in formation over the Palace. You must be feeling very proud.

JUNE (*as Mrs Miller*). Proud and honoured.

JENNIFER (*to Mrs Miller's doll children*). Your daddy will be leading the squadron, June. He'll be flying the legendary Battle of Britain Memorial Hurricane.

JUNE (*as Mrs Miller's daughter*). The Queen will be watching from the balcony of Buckingham Palace. The Queen and the Royal Family.

JUNE (*as Mrs Miller*). Here she comes.

(*As the Queen's carriage passes*). Isn't her golden carriage wonderful!

We hear the hooves of the eight white horses drawing the Queen's golden carriage.

JENNIFER (*off-script*). Her golden carriage drawn by eight white horses. At this point I would like to point out to our listeners at home that the horses are white. All white, manes, tails –

JUNE (*hissing*). That bit's cut.

JENNIFER. – everything. Like unicorns. Pegasuses –

JUNE. Stop it.

JENNIFER. – pulling Cinderella's carriage through a forest of people, twenty, maybe thirty deep –

JUNE sings the sound of pealing bells to shut JENNIFER up.

JUNE. Those are the Bow Bells we hear.

(*Whispers.*) The red carpet.

JENNIFER rolls a length of red ribbon between the rows of dolls.

Then a shorter length across the top to make a cross.

As they pull up to St Paul's Cathedral, you can't see this at home, ladies and gentleman, but Her Majesty is radiant. She takes the beefeater's hand and leaves the carriage.

JUNE takes the Queen out of the carriage.

(*Pointedly.*) The Duke always behind her.

JENNIFER takes the Duke out of the carriage.

The Duke walks behind the Queen up the red carpet, as both girls sing 'Jerusalem'.

JENNIFER (*reading from her miniscule script as the Vicar*). Our nation and commonwealth, those millions of people throughout the world, have been blessed beyond measure by having at our heart an example of service untiringly done and a home life stable and wonderfully happy.

JUNE (*interrupting*). And now the moment we've all been waiting for: the Queen.

(*As the Queen.*) When I was twenty-one I pledged my life to the service of our people, both here and throughout the commonwealth, and I asked God's help to make good that vow –

JENNIFER (*looking at her watch*). We should cut to the balcony.

JUNE. Although that vow was in my salad days, when I was green in judgement, I do not regret nor detract / one word of it.

JENNIFER. It's better to skip straight to the balcony. The planes are heading towards the Palace. Flying above the rooftops of London like a flock of gigantic / birds...

JUNE (*interrupting*). We are now on the balcony of Buckingham Palace.

The Queen has been joined by the Queen Mother in yellow chiffon.

/ Canary yellow.

JENNIFER. Like a flock of gigantic birds due to arrive here at the Palace any minute / now.

JUNE. Princess Margaret in deeper pink is beside her sister / the Queen.

JENNIFER. Listen. I can hear the noise of planes –

JUNE. The Duchess of Kent looking resplendent in lime green.

JENNIFER. I can hear the sound of engines.

JUNE. The Queen's daughter Anne is also wearing / green.

JENNIFER. They're getting nearer –

JUNE. Not robust lime like the Duchess, but a more demure, sombre / mint –

JENNIFER. And here they come –

JUNE. – as befits her present condition.

JENNIFER (*standing*). We see the first plane flying over the palace.

JUNE, *relaxing as* JENNIFER *takes lead, uses her script to shield her eyes.*

JUNE. The Royal Family shield their eyes as they look to the skies.

JENNIFER. Up above them, Mrs Miller's husband, the Flight Commander, leading the formation in his Battle of Britain Memorial Flight Hurricane.

JUNE. The Royal Family are applauding.

JENNIFER. June and Jennifer Miller wave to their father.

We hear the planes fly over.

JUNE *is waving and calling towards the sky, her face luminous.*

JUNE. Daddy. My daddy.

Her movements are slowed down like a moment in a film.

JENNIFER. What a magnificent end to a perfect day.

We listen to the planes disappear into the distance.

JENNIFER *turns the tape off.*

The Generation Game *is turned up downstairs to let the girls know to come down.*

GLORIA (*calling from the stairs*). Hurry up before your tea grow cold.

Generation Game started.

JENNIFER. Didn't we do well.

The TWINS *head for the bedroom door.*

The Generation Game *plays into the unit at Eastgate.*

September 1977. Eastgate

A room in the Special Unit at the Eastgate Centre.

The visit is for GLORIA *and the* TWINS *to meet* CATHY ARTHUR *before starting at the unit.*

GLORIA *is dressed as before in coat, hat, matching handbag and gloves.*

The TWINS *are wearing their school uniforms.*

CATHY, *in jeans and T-shirt, two months pregnant, hurries in carrying armfuls of 'stuff'.*

CATHY. Come in! Come in! Welcome. Have a seat. Make yourselves at home. Take off your coats.

GLORIA *sits on the offered chair.*

She removes her hat and gloves and places them on her lap.

She talks with her clipped West Indian telephone voice.

The TWINS *stand behind* GLORIA, *in formal photograph pose throughout.*

They stare straight ahead.

Occasionally they move slowly in unison to adjust their posture and position.

CATHY *doesn't sit down.*

Can I get you a drink? Tea? Coffee?

(*To the* TWINS.) Juice?

GLORIA. No, thank you. We're fine. Thank you.

CATHY. Thank you for coming to see me today. I know how hard it can be to come to a new place where everything's different. Everyone's new. I know that you had a difficult time at your last school so we hope that you'll feel welcome here.

Here we create a relaxed environment. You will be seen as individuals. We don't have a uniform. You can wear your own clothes. And call us by our Christian names –

GLORIA. What them supposed to wear, Mrs…?

CATHY. Cathy. Call me Cathy.

GLORIA. What them to wear, Miss Catherine?

CATHY. Well, that's up to June and Jennifer.

However you feel most comfortable.

We want you to know that we're here for you.

To help support you,

and your family…

to move forward –

GLORIA. How many hours a day, Mrs...?

CATHY. Cathy. Call me Cathy.

GLORIA. What time do they finish?

CATHY. We follow school hours. But we allow the children to create their own timetable according to their needs. We value the unique qualities of every child and the choices they make. We encourage the children to express themselves in whatever way / they choose.

GLORIA. How long before they can return to Sir Thomas Picton Secondary Modern?

CATHY. Well, that depends on what's best for / June and for Jennifer...

GLORIA. Their father want them back in education soon as possible. Want them taking their examination. Getting their certificate. The twinnies want to follow them sister to secretarial school.

CATHY. I think we need to take things a step at a time. June and Jennifer have been through a difficult, a distressing experience –

GLORIA *gets to her feet.*

GLORIA. If that's all, we'd better be on our way. Their father get home five thirty. Him like his tea ready and waiting.

CATHY (*to the* TWINS). Do you have any questions. Anything you'd like to know before we begin next week?

GLORIA. They'll be here nine o'clock on Monday... in their uniform.

GLORIA *leaves.*

JUNE. *I blame the daffodils. Who wants to hear summery sounds? Not me. I hate summer. The same old outings, happy people going on long-planned holidays. Children sucking ice cream, pregnant women wearing blousey dresses. Why can't it be winter the whole year round? Do we really need summer?*

Lights change.

September 1977. Mr Nobody

A hot September day at the Eastgate Centre.

A fly is buzzing.

CATHY. Today I'm going to find out some more about Jennifer
and June. I know that you live on the RAF base with your
mum and dad. I know that you have two sisters and a brother.
I usually do this one-to-one but I'm wondering if you'd rather
not be apart. So I've brought with me some boxes. Each one
represents a member of your family.

CATHY *names the boxes as she places them on the floor in
front of the* TWINS.

Dad.

Mum.

Recently married Greta. The oldest.

Then David who just started college.

June and Jennifer, of course.

And the baby of the family, Rosie.

This box is called Mr Nobody.

I'm going to put him over here on his own.

I'm going to ask you questions.

You post the question into one of the boxes to show me your
answer.

You don't have to speak.

Unless you want to.

All you have to do is put the question into the box.

Are you sure you don't want to take your blazers off?

Neither TWIN *replies or moves.*

CATHY *reads aloud a question.*

Who makes you laugh?

CATHY *hands each* TWIN *a slip of paper with the question written on it.*

The TWINS *shyly titter.*

Then slyly the TWINS *eye each other to see if they are playing.*

Tentatively they lift their slip in unison.

They read silently in unison.

Slowly they venture forward, each aware of the other.

In unison they post their slip into Rosie's box.

Rosie makes you both laugh.

In unison they walk back towards CATHY *and turn to stare at the boxes.*

CATHY *puts a slip into their hands.*

Who comforts you when you are sad?

Out of the corner of their eyes, both TWINS *eye each other.*

They walk to the boxes in unison.

In unison they post their slip into their mum's box.

Mum comforts you when you're sad.

In unison they walk back towards CATHY.

CATHY *gives them a slip.*

Who do you go to when you need to talk?

Both TWINS *eye each other out of the corner of their eyes.*

They are uncomfortable, unsure as to whether to answer.

After a few moments they walk to the boxes in unison.

They post their slips into each other's boxes.

JENNIFER *goes to* JUNE, *and* JUNE *goes to* JENNIFER.

Who understands you the best?

CATHY *gives* JUNE *and* JENNIFER *a slip.*

JUNE *and* JENNIFER *cross to the boxes.*

JENNIFER *goes to post her slip into* JUNE*'s box.*

JUNE *has hesitated and is standing frozen holding her slip.*

After several seconds' hesitation they post their slip into each other's boxes.

Who do you tell your secrets to?

CATHY *offers them the new question slips.*

JENNIFER *is about to take the slip.*

JENNIFER *grabs both slips and crumples them in her fist.*

There is enormous tension.

Okay. I'm sorry. I can see that this is difficult.

Let's leave it for today.

I've brought some pictures in to show you.

Pictures of animals.

CATHY *gets a copy of* National Geographic *from her bag.*

Animals and birds, from where you come from… where your parents come from. From an island in the Caribbean. The rainforest. We're going to have a look at the pictures together. We're going to imagine what it's like to be free like these animals. Then I want you to write me a story.

Lights change.

Dallas

The TWINS *are in their bedroom.*

There is tension in the silent room.

JENNIFER *climbs onto her top bunk and starts writing.*

JUNE. Come on. It's Friday. It's 'Cooking on a Budget Day'.

You can be Delia.

I'll let you be Delia.

JUNE *begins to arrange the dolls around the radio.*

Mrs Miller has invited all her friends round.

All the RAF wives.

Look, everybody's come. Everybody's ready.

You can be Delia?

Everybody's waiting.

They've got to get home to cook tea before *Dallas*.

Mrs Miller will need to prepare June and Jennifer's dinner.

JENNIFER *begins to scribble furiously into the notepad she takes from under her pillow.*

JUNE *gets her home-made microphone.*

Welcome. Good evening. And hello.

Today, we are back with Delia.

JUNE *thrusts the microphone towards* JENNIFER, *leaping up to try to make her laugh.*

We are concentrating on the family pudding.

So, Delia Dimplebottom, you're saying if we use Nimble to make bread and butter pudding, we'll still fly like a bird in the sky.

JUNE *squeezes her face and the microphone in front of* JENNIFER.

JUNE *sings the theme tune from the 'Nimble' TV advert.*

JENNIFER (*suddenly erupting*). Once there was two parrots who were brought up to live in a zoo. Every day people would come to the zoo and see the parrots. Sometimes the parrots would mock the talking people and sometimes they would have a conversation between themselves. The parrots often talked how they longed to get back to their native land.

Sometimes they would ask the watchers to open the cage door and let them out. The people would laugh and think the parrots were kidding. Some of the children who were watching asked their parents if they could take the parrots home.

Before the parents had time to answer one parrot would say: 'We're not for sale.' And the other parrot would say the same.

The Dallas *theme is turned up downstairs to let the* TWINS *know to come down.*

JUNE *climbs up to* JENNIFER*'s bunk.*

JUNE. Lucy's bringing her parents home today.

Valene and Gary are coming to Southfork.

I need to see what Sue Ellen's wearing.

JUNE *is pulling the bedclothes.*

JENNIFER *is holding them tight.*

They wrestle with the duvet until JENNIFER *slumps back onto the bed, playing dead.*

Don't do this.

Not tonight.

JUNE *tries to lift the inert* JENNIFER.

The Dallas *theme tune ends.*

JUNE, *frantic, drags* JENNIFER*'s inert body over the edge of the bunk beds and to the floor.*

I can hear them talking. We're missing the plot. We're missing the story. We won't know what's happened.

They are both on the floor. JUNE *struggles with* JENNIFER's *inert body.*

JUNE *pulls deadweight* JENNIFER *towards her.*

JUNE *pushes and pulls* JENNIFER *across the room in a vain attempt to get her to the door.*

You bitch.

I'm missing *Dallas* because of you.

Everyone else will know what's happened.

Valene, and Gary, and Lucy, and Sue Ellen's dress.

I can hear JR.

GLORIA, *in her buttoned-up housecoat, comes in.*

GLORIA. You want the popcorn go floppy. *Dallas* already start.

What's going on in here?

I say what a go on.

JENNIFER *gets to her feet, staring at* JUNE, *and leaves the room to go downstairs.*

Lights change.

Jelly Babies

The Eastgate Centre.

CATHY. I know from your mother that you speak to her, and although you haven't spoken to anyone here at the unit in the two months since you arrived, you talk when alone together at home. I also know from your mother that you are both fond of jelly babies.

CATHY *takes a packet of jelly babies and places them on the floor in front of the* TWINS.

Today we're going to begin a conversation.

Nothing complicated.

Just introductions.

The first step. That's all.

You get one jelly baby for a 'hello'.

One word. That's all I'm asking for.

The TWINS *cross their arms in unison.*

Why not?

Why not try it?

What is there to lose?

What could happen that would be so terrible?

The TWINS *both look away.*

CATHY *takes a file from her bag.*

Very well.

We'll return to the photographs of people we were looking at yesterday.

We were talking about how we express our feelings. This time I want you to put them into two piles. In this pile I want you to put the people you think are happy and in this pile the ones you think are…

JUNE. Hello.

CATHY *looks at* JUNE.

JUNE *looks away.*

Thank you.

Thank you, June.

Well done.

That wasn't so bad, was it?

CATHY *waits for* JUNE *to acknowledge what she has just achieved.*

That wasn't so terrible?

CATHY *puts a jelly baby into* JUNE's *hand.*

JUNE *opens her hand to receive the jelly baby.*

Eat it before it gets sticky.

Jennifer, would you like one too?

I'll give you one for a 'hello'.

(*Coaxing.*) Two for a 'hello' with a smile.

JUNE. Hello.

CATHY. Hello. I'm June.

JUNE (*quietly*). Hello. I'm June.

CATHY. Can you say it louder?

Can you say it so that we can hear you?

JUNE. Hello I'm June.

CATHY. You want people to know your name, don't you?

What will we call you if we don't know your name?

The twinnies?

Is that who you are?

Is that who you want to be for the rest of your life?

JUNE. June. I'm June.

CATHY. Well done.

CATHY *takes a jelly baby from the packet.*

She puts it into JUNE*'s hand. As she does she hears a voice.*

JENNIFER (*quietly*). Jennifer.

CATHY *turns to face* JENNIFER.

CATHY *gives* JENNIFER *a jelly baby.*

CATHY. Hello. I'm Jennifer.

JENNIFER. Hello. I'm 'nifer.

CATHY *gives* JUNE *a jelly baby.*

CATHY. Hello. I'm Jennifer. This is my sister, June.

JENNIFER. I'm Jennifer.

JUNE. Sister Jennifer.

I am June.

CATHY. Thank you.

Good. Very good.

(*To* JUNE.) I'm going to give you two jelly babies because you told me your sister's name as well as your own.

CATHY *gives* JUNE *two jelly babies.*

She looks directly at JUNE.

This time I want you to look at me. I want you to tell me your name. Not just say it but tell me. Talk to me. Cathy. Tell me who you are. I want to know who you are, June. I'll give you the packet. You can have them all. All you have to do is look at me and they're yours.

CATHY *holds out the packet to* JUNE.

Look at me, June.

Just as JUNE *is about to look at* CATHY, JENNIFER *is heard whispering furiously.*

JENNIFER. You are Jennifer.

You are me.

JUNE. I am June.

Beat.

CATHY. Well done.

JENNIFER *suddenly turns on* CATHY, *wild with rage.*

She grabs the bag of jelly babies, her face inches away from CATHY*'s.*

Well done, Jennifer.

Lights change.

Eating Jelly Babies

The TWINS' *bedroom.*

JENNIFER *takes the packet of jelly babies and stuffs* JUNE's *face into it.*

JUNE *struggles to free herself.*

For several moments it is as if JENNIFER *is going to suffocate* JUNE.

Finally, JENNIFER *releases* JUNE, *who is coughing and choking.*

JUNE *stands aloof, breathing hard.*

A few feet away, JENNIFER *kneels down.*

JENNIFER *opens the bag of jelly babies.*

She shares the exact same number of sweets into parallel lines on the carpet.

She looks at JUNE.

After a moment, JUNE *comes to kneel facing her.*

In unison, keeping their eyes on each other, the TWINS *put a jelly baby into their mouths.*

The speed they put the jelly babies into their mouths increases until they are cramming.

GLORIA *enters the bedroom, carrying the Littlewoods catalogue.*

GLORIA. Greta drop the Littlewoods catalogue today. Come down, come choose something for Christmas? You need to pick out your presents for the family. Best to order early and avoid the rush. They have them new shoe with the platform heel Greta wear at her wedding.

No response.

What you want to eat?

No response.

Fish fingers, beans, bread, no crusts?

Angel Delight. Mint choc chip.

No response.

Me turn the telly up so you know when *Pop a de Top* start.

GLORIA *leaves.*

JENNIFER. She's been crying again.

JUNE. I saw an envelope on the mat.

JENNIFER. More begging from back home.

JUNE. She wants to go home.

JENNIFER. How d'you know?

JUNE *checks that* GLORIA *is not listening at the door.*

JUNE. I heard them when I was in the toilet. He said she needs to try harder.

She speaks too strong, no wonder no one understands her. He told her to have coffee mornings. Tupperware parties for the RAF wives. She said she'd sent out invitations but everyone's busy.

JENNIFER (*imitating her father's West Indian accent as if doing something unallowed*). Them always busy. Me a watch the cricket.

JUNE (*imitating their mother*). You always watching cricket. You marry to the cricket.

They laugh, nervously.

JENNIFER. Is a man not allowed to watch television in his own house? You want me miss the score. No, better still me a go watch the game in peace. In the club me can hear meself tink.

JUNE. Don't come back, you hear, for all the good you do sitting in that chair, your eyes like box. We don't even go to church since you watch *Songs of Praise* on the BBC. You must think God there inna the television. You stare at screen all day air-traffic control and then you come home do the same. No wonder your daughters don't speak.

Beat.

JENNIFER. Them nah speak cos a you. It take a white woman to learn them.

Silence.

The TWINS *look at one another.*

JUNE. Wolmer's School for Boys, Kingston, Jamaica, taught you the kings and queens of Hingland. Them taught you the name of every city and what that city famous fi make. You know every railroad. The stations. Even the name of the parks, the streets, the monuments of London. I know I didn't win a scholarship to wear fancy blue blazer, to sit desk by desk with the Prime Minister Michael Norman Manley to learn Greek and Latin. I don't have no certificate in my hand. No failed dreams of RAF pilot. But what I do know is we don't fit here.

JENNIFER. Back home: you no even have cooker, let alone toilet. Any life is a better life fi you.

JUNE. Go on, go to the club. You think I care?

Pressing their ears to the floor, they speak in their own voices.

You think she be all right?

JENNIFER. If she goes home we have to go with her.

JUNE. No cooker. No toilet… No television.

The TWINS *look at one another.*

JENNIFER *speaks with a BBC radio-presenter voice into a pretend microphone.*

She wants to make her sister laugh.

JENNIFER (*RP accent*). If you are having trouble with your West Indian husband, make him some goat. Curried, preferably.

JUNE (*RP accent*). When delivering his dinner, do not under any account get in the way of the television which will undoubtedly be playing cricket.

JENNIFER. If unwanted during cricket hours.

JUNE. Feeling unwanted, that is.

Do invite your white friends.

JUNE *picks up the Barbie doll that is Mrs Miller.*

JENNIFER. Friends and acquaintances, over for a Tupperware party. (*Putting the microphone to Mrs Miller's lips.*) Mrs Miller, could you, please?

JUNE (*as Mrs Miller*). The essential of any Tupperware party is…

JENNIFER…. a plastic tub.

JUNE. Here's one we bought earlier.

JENNIFER. Notice how the lid clasps shut.

JUNE. Like so.

JENNIFER. Good for storing the recently removed bollocks of said troublesome West Indian husband.

JUNE. They can be later chilled.

JENNIFER. Or even frozen.

JUNE. For a Tupperware party do not, however, wear back-a-yard clothing. Do not wear yellow nylon.

Do not wear frills.

JENNIFER. A real RAF wife wears A-line skirts. Marks and Spencer's. Demure blouses.

JUNE. She does not dress herself up like a Christmas tree to be in her own house.

JENNIFER. Do, however, get out the good china.

JUNE. But don't lift your little finger.

JENNIFER. Or use your telephone voice.

JUNE. This week we are promoting, as an accompaniment for table-to-fridge Tupperware, that will complement your hostess trolley, the delectable Lazy Susan.

JENNIFER. So lazy she can barely get out of bed.

JUNE. The Lazy Susan – a must for every family. No more fights about what's put where on the table. Just spin the dish and your favourite food comes to you.

JENNIFER. Vol-au-vents and Twiglets as much as you wish.

JUNE (*listening*). I can hear *Top of the Pops*. It's five past *Top of the Pops*.

JENNIFER. She hasn't turned the telly up.

JUNE. Six past.

JENNIFER. She didn't turn the telly up.

JUNE. What's she doing?

> *They go to the door and peer out into the darkness of the landing.*

What do you think she's doing?

She hasn't even made us any food.

I'm hungry.

Drumsticks

The Eastgate Centre.

CATHY *brings a drum and drumsticks into the room.*

The TWINS *stand in the middle of the room.*

As CATHY *speaks, they slowly turn away from her.*

CATHY. I wanted to start by saying how pleased I was with the progress made last week. And to say thank you... thank you to you both for...

> CATHY *walks around in front of the* TWINS.

Thank you for making that first step towards...

> *The* TWINS *turn away again.*

> *As* CATHY *speaks, she positions herself in front of them again.*

I understand, I know how difficult it must have been.

The TWINS *slowly turn away.*

Today we're really going to make some noise.

CATHY *tries to put a drumstick into* JENNIFER*'s hand.*

The drumstick slides out of JENNIFER*'s limp fingers and falls to the floor.*

CATHY *tries again, but* JENNIFER *refuses to grasp the drumstick.*

CATHY *tries again.*

And again.

CATHY*'s frustration is getting the better of her.*

The TWINS *stand motionless.*

CATHY *walks away and tries to gather herself.*

She turns back to the TWINS.

I've decided it's time for a change of scene. We're going to get out of the unit. We're going to go on a day trip. We're going on an adventure. And I want you to choose where we go. The funfair, the castle, the theatre. We could go and see *The Snow Queen*, the Christmas show at the Palace. It's about a little boy who gets captured and taken away from his family to a white land of snow and ice because a splinter of glass gets into his heart and makes him so cold that he can't... he doesn't know how to... he forgets. He doesn't even recognise his own sister... And afterwards we can see the Christmas lights, and the Littlewoods windows and...

She catches her breath.

I'm going to leave you with a pen and paper. You tell me. Tell me please what you want.

CATHY *leaves.*

Lights change.

Christmas

The sound of a radio playing Christmas carols.

The TWINS *sing along to 'Silent Night'.*

JENNIFER *is straightening out the branches of their tiny artificial Christmas tree.*

JUNE *is doing the finishing touches to Mrs Miller's Christmas outfit.*

JENNIFER *places the tree in the middle of the room.*

JUNE *arranges presents around the tree.*

JUNE, JENNIFER, *Mrs Miller and all the RAF-wife Barbies sit around the tree and presents.*

GLORIA *enters.*

GLORIA. Happy Christmas, my darlings. Happy Christmas. The fire is lit. The candles them burning. The tree all glitter, glitter. The presents them stack. The breakfast ready fi serve. Bacon, sausage and a whole heap a eggs. You no hear Greta and she husband knock five minutes since?

GLORIA *has begun gathering the five big presents from beneath the* TWINS' *tree.*

And your father buy a whole pack a Babycham for him big gals. And eggnog. You can make a snowball. Luxury. A little tipple first thing a morning.

GLORIA *tries to put a parcel into* JENNIFER's *hand.*

Jennifer, you want me drop it?

The parcel slides out of JENNIFER's *limp fingers and falls to the floor.*

June, you carry this one. To Greta and her husband Philip. That's nice. I know she'll appreciate it. I can carry these three. I can't carry everything. June, just carry this little one.

GLORIA *tries to put the parcel into* JUNE's *limp fingers.*

JUNE *refuses to grasp the parcel.*

GLORIA *looks at the* TWINS.

It's Christmas. Day in, day out you're up here. It's Christmas. Just for the day, you wrote. You wrote so in my Christmas card. You promised. June.

JUNE *looks at* JENNIFER, *who looks away.*

Your father, your big sister, her husband, your brother, me and little Rosie are sat round the table a wait. You intend to spoil it. You intend to spoil Christmas for everyone?

JENNIFER *starts to hum 'Silent Night' as she sits down beside the Christmas tree.* JUNE *is caught between her mother and sister.*

(*Suddenly.*) Think of everything me a do for you. Every day cooking and washing and running up and down them stair. Never so much as a word. All I'm asking you come down open your presents. Please. Don't show your father up in front of Greta's husband. Not in front of the white boy.

JENNIFER *looks towards the tiny Christmas tree.*

JENNIFER. Everything's ready. Everyone's here. It's nearly time to open the presents.

JENNIFER *looks at* JUNE.

JUNE *looks at* GLORIA.

GLORIA *looks at* JENNIFER.

GLORIA. It's the last me ever beg of you.

JENNIFER *turns away, humming a Christmas carol.*

JUNE *follows her to the Christmas tree.*

GLORIA *leaves with the large presents, leaving the door open.*

JUNE. We said we'd go downstairs.

She's upset.

We promised.

Like always. Every year.

JENNIFER. They can read the labels.

JUNE. That's what we do.

JENNIFER. They've got their names on.

JUNE. We'll miss the Queen's speech.

JENNIFER. We can listen to it on the radio.

JUNE. Just for the day, we said. You said so. I want to see their faces when they open them. Take pictures with Greta's Polaroid Camera. I want to play David's Twister, and Rosie's Buckeroo.

JENNIFER. It's up to you. You have to choose. You can have today with them or you can go to *The Snow Queen* with Cathy.

JUNE. I can do what I like.

JENNIFER. Really. I won't go with you. And you won't go on your own. Choose.

JUNE. I want to see *The Snow Queen* at the theatre with Cathy. I want to see the Christmas lights and the Littlewoods windows and the funfair and the castle.

JENNIFER *locks the door.*

Lights change.

I lack something but it's not love. I love Rosie, David, Greta and Phil, Mom and Dad. I worry about my mother. I see grief for all those years in her eyes. She is not young, but she is romantic, a child at heart. I cannot bear to die before my parents, to walk on the graves of my parents, put down flowers and feel lost.

March 1978

The Eastgate Centre

CATHY, *heavily pregnant, sits opposite* GLORIA, *dressed as before in her best coat and hat.*

Throughout the scene, JUNE *and* JENNIFER *are slowly putting away the dolls' Christmas.*

CATHY. It's been a while since we last spoke… and I thought it might be useful to touch base… find out how things are at home for the twins… and for you…

GLORIA. Me?

CATHY. The family.

GLORIA. Greta's baby christening Sunday. Philip. We call him after him daddy. He's the family now.

CATHY. As you know, I'm soon going to be taking maternity leave –

GLORIA. I wanted to ask you, Miss Catherine, what progress them making here? You say last time we meet them started talking. Them talking to you?

CATHY. Yes. That's right. They were.

GLORIA. How much longer do you think it will take before they're ready to return / to school?

CATHY. It's true, when we last met I thought I was winning their trust, that it was only a matter of time before the twins would abandon their silence… But, I have to be honest with you, Mrs Gibbons. I wish I could tell you that the twins were making progress, but they seem to be withdrawing deeper into themselves –

GLORIA. You take them to the theatre.

CATHY. Yes / I did.

GLORIA. To the funfair. Them come back with two coconuts and a teddy bear.

CATHY. That's right.

GLORIA. You say them talking.

CATHY. I did.

GLORIA. You tell me them talking to you.

CATHY. They were.

GLORIA. How did them win two coconuts and a teddy bear?

CATHY. I did. I won them. I gave them to them... to you, I mean. I'm afraid they... they wouldn't look... wouldn't lift their eyes from their feet. I kept thinking, surely, surely they'll give in. They won't be able to resist.

GLORIA is staring at CATHY.

I sometimes try to imagine. What would it be like? At school I was always the one who got into trouble for talking. I had to stand in a corner with my face to the wall. What was that party game? The one where you had to see how long you could be silent. I couldn't do it. I'd be desperate to say something. Make a noise. As if I'd burst if I didn't. As if I didn't exist.

Can you imagine, Mrs Gibbons? Can you imagine what it must be like? Not to be able to ask for anything or share your thoughts or explain what you mean or make someone understand...

Pause.

I'm sorry. I'm very sorry. I –

GLORIA stands suddenly and heads for the door.

Mrs Gibbons... Gloria...

Lights change.

In the half-light we see KENNEDY, *a young American teenager, circling on his bicycle.*

He stops and lights a cigarette/joint, taking a long slow drag, and blowing smoke into the air.

Goodbye

CATHY *is standing in front of the* TWINS, *holding two leather-bound diaries*.

CATHY. As you know, I'm going to be leaving to have my baby. I wanted to give you something, something to remember me by.

KENNEDY *strolls into the room*.

Kennedy, do you mind.

KENNEDY. No, not at all.

CATHY. This is June and Jennifer's session.

KENNEDY. Of course.

KENNEDY *sits on the edge of the space on his bike, chewing and watching the* TWINS.

CATHY *places a diary into the hands of each of the* TWINS.

CATHY. I wish you all the luck in the world.

And I know you wish me luck with the baby.

CATHY *leaves*.

JUNE *starts to cry silently*.

She lifts her arm to cover her face.

JENNIFER *pulls at her arm*.

JUNE *pushes her away*.

This turns into a tussle as JUNE *tries to hide her face and* JENNIFER *tries to stop her*.

JENNIFER *tries to smother* JUNE *to stop her from crying*.

JENNIFER *wrestles* JUNE *to the floor*.

She kneels on JUNE's *elbows so she is pinioned to the ground and cannot hide her face*.

JENNIFER (*furious. Hissing in her ear*). Stop it. Stop it. You are Jennifer. You are Jennifer. You are me.

KENNEDY *picks up one of the diaries from the floor.*

KENNEDY. What's up, skinny black rabbits?

The TWINS *freeze.*

KENNEDY *flicks open his lighter and puts the flame to the edge of a page.*

The page starts to burn.

I know you're fucking mad but surely you're not fucking stupid as well. That uptight bitch didn't care about yer. She didn't give a jackshit about yer. She was using yer for her research. We're her research. We're her chance to show every fucker how clever she is. We paid her fucking mortgage. We're paying for her fucking baby-stroller. She was always gonna leave.

KENNEDY *drops the burning book.*

He comes over to the TWINS *and breathes in* JENNIFER'*s ear as he speaks.*

You're outsiders like me in this little horror-movie town.

KENNEDY *leaves on his bike, dropping his chewing gum.*

JENNIFER *releases* JUNE *and scrabbles on the floor for the gum.*

She picks up KENNEDY'*s chewing gum and smells it, breathing in the scent of him.*

She puts it into her mouth and chews.

JUNE. *All through my schooldays I got a strange feeling I was a boy. It's as though I'd been a boy first in my life. It wasn't anything like masturbation. But it had to be done in secret. I would get my mum's Littlewoods catalogue. I was filled with anger, rage and jealousy that a man would actually get turned on by women in the nude, and an intense hate for those models; those senseless, feminine, defenceless women. The humiliation I would have to suffer as a female. All this because of Eve and that forbidden fruit. Women were to be degraded for all their life through.*

Lights change.

The Art of Conversation

JUNE, *in her bedroom, is reading* Matchmaker *magazine.*

JUNE. 'Romantic male seeks loving female for long walks, star gazing and sweet talk. Must be quiet, home-loving and attractive.'

We hear GLORIA *knocking on the door.*

GLORIA. Parcel for you.

JUNE. It's here.

JENNIFER *opens the door using the key and brings in a parcel, locking the door behind her.*

JUNE *unwraps the parcel.*

JUNE *starts to read.*

'*The Art of Conversation.* Techniques for beginning. Beginning can be the hardest part of any conversation, especially when you're nervous. A few simple tips will make all the difference to your performance. Follow our rules and see how easy it is to make that all-important first step.'

JENNIFER. We'll try it on Kennedy.

JUNE (*reading the chapter headings*). 'Greetings. Openers. Anecdotes. Questions. Ping-pong.'

JENNIFER. Ping-pong?

JUNE (*finding the page*). 'Don't talk too long without pausing for reaction. More than a minute is usually too long. Forty seconds is ideal. Aim to generate the "ping-pong" effect. An easy way to achieve this is to ask a question. Get ready for your date by thinking of interesting questions. What are their hobbies and special interests? Do they have any pets? Do they like to cook? Or play a musical instrument?'

JENNIFER. Let's try it on Kennedy.

JUNE. 'Do they support a football team? What's their favourite sport?'

JENNIFER *unlocks the door and gets the phone from the hallway.*

JENNIFER *dials.*

KENNEDY *enters as he picks up the receiver.*

The TWINS *are listening as he speaks.*

KENNEDY. Chief Officer George Kennedy's residence. If you wanna talk to my daddy, he's out there on parade all dressed up in his uniform, doing as he's told. You want to speak to my mommy, she killed herself, so she won't be coming to the phone today. My stepmother is out having a manicure. You want to leave her a message?

Silence.

Who the fuck is that?

The TWINS *slam down the receiver.*

Lights change.

The Writing School

JENNIFER. *Please God, let me be bold enough to speak openly. I have been a soul with no hope. Don't let this disease paralyse me, destroying my abilities, tying up my tongue like firewood.*

The TWINS *are in their bedroom.*

JUNE *is composing a letter to* Matchmaker *magazine.*

JUNE. 'Students, June and Jennifer, aged fifteen. Enjoy music, poetry and dancing.'

Is that enough?

JENNIFER. Reading?

JUNE. 'Enjoy music – (*Writing.*) writing, reading, poetry and dancing. Requires shy males aged sixteen to twenty.' (*Thinks for a moment.*) Or sixteen to twenty-five?

41

JENNIFER. Sixteen to twenty.

JUNE. 'Requires shy males aged sixteen to twenty-five for correspondence. (*Reading back what she has written*.) Must be emotional, sensitive, compassionnate, romantic, reliable, mature, serious and honest.'

JENNIFER. Compatibility with Aries essential.

(*Reading the magazine*.) It says we have to send a photo.

How we gonna send a photo?

JUNE (*continuing to write*). 'Any nationality welcome.'

JENNIFER. I said, how are we gonna send a photo? We can't send a photo.

JUNE. With David's camera. We can use Greta's hot comb to straighten our hair. Borrow her Fade Out Cream.

JENNIFER. They don't work.

JUNE. It'll make our skin look lighter. Look paler.

JENNIFER. It's never worked on her.

JUNE. It has.

JENNIFER. Are you blind?

JUNE (*getting upset*). We have to send a photograph. 'Your application to *Matchmaker* magazine will not be processed unless you send a photograph.'

JENNIFER. Nobody will want us. They won't choose us...

JUNE. We can wear pink lipstick.

JENNIFER. Your face is fat whatever you do. Fat and flat and ugly.

JUNE. Just like yours.

JENNIFER *goes to grab the copy of* Matchmaker *magazine.*

There is a fierce tussle as JENNIFER *tears the magazine to pieces.*

JUNE *gathers the torn, crumpled magazine and tries to piece it back together again.*

She lifts a crumpled advert from the pile.

She stands up.

JENNIFER *is watching.*

Beat.

(*Reading.*) 'The Writing School. Become a professional author. Eighty pounds per pupil. Money back guaranteed if not satisfied.' Forty each if we enroll as one. We can save up. Become writers.

JENNIFER. Authors.

JUNE. When we're famous, everyone will want us.

Lights change.

JENNIFER. *The day will have to come when we are both talking, moving fast, laughing, living. I will gain control, control over my mind and my body. I will gain control.*

The TWINS *are sitting on the bedroom floor with The Writing School manual.*

JUNE *reads aloud.*

JUNE (*reading*). 'Dear Student 8201, thank you for enrolling with The Writing School. We hope you will enjoy your journey towards becoming a professional writer.

Words are the writer's most important tool. Like notes on the stave, the more we can play, the greater the possibilities for our music. Set yourself the task of learning four new words every day. Choose words that inspire and will enhance your powers of description.'

Lights change.

The TWINS *are testing one another on the meanings of words they have learnt.*

JUNE. Atone.

JENNIFER. Make amends. Expiate. Repair.

Atrocity.

JUNE. A wicked or cruel act involving extreme violence or injury.

Atrophy.

JENNIFER. Waste away through undernourishment or lack of use. Become emaciated, starved, cut off from all source of sustenance.

Lights change.

JENNIFER. Synonym.

JUNE. A word that is suggestive of, or associated with, another.

JENNIFER. Simile.

JUNE. Something that is used to describe another entity. A seeming likeness. A reflection upon. That which holds a mirror revealing the nature of the object itself.

Lights change.

Reading from the manual.

'Although there may be many twists and turns along the way, a successful plot must end by tying up all loose ends and subsidiary elements, including your subplot. The reader will experience a sense of satisfaction as the pieces come together like a jigsaw to create one harmonious whole.'

During the following speech, KENNEDY *can be seen at home dialling a phone number.*

He is listening to a news report on the television.

'Do not underestimate the importance of the subplot. Whilst your key characters occupy the foreground of your novel, there should be other more shadowy individuals who exist to add contrast, intrigue and colour to your story.'

In the background of the speech we can hear the sound of the phone ringing downstairs. We see GLORIA *picking it up.*

GLORIA. Hello.

KENNEDY. Hello. Can I speak to June and Jennifer, please?

GLORIA. Just one moment, please.

> (*Calling upstairs, excited.*) Twinnies, there's a young man on the telephone.

> GLORIA *stands looking on as* JUNE *picks up the receiver and hands it to* JENNIFER.

> KENNEDY *opens a can of beer whilst holding the phone with his chin.*

> *The spray from the can creates a fountain.*

> *He speaks slowly as if he's been smoking cannabis.*

> *The* TWINS *are both listening as he speaks.*

> *In the background we can hear the television news report.*

KENNEDY. Goggle the box, man. Loads of fellow jungle bunnies are torching Brixton.

> *The* TWINS *listen, excited.*

> I know you two crazies are listening. I can hear you breathing. I can hear you fucking panting.

GLORIA. Go on, speak to him.

KENNEDY. Don't think I don't know it's you that's been calling me for months. Don't think I don't know what's going on in those fucked-up heads of yours. I can see your window. I've seen your curtain twitching.

> You like what you see, huh?

GLORIA. Say something!

KENNEDY. You want to come here and try it? Find out what you've been missing all these years.

GLORIA. Ask him round for tea.

KENNEDY. I can blow your fucking minds.

GLORIA. Tell him come Sunday. Me bake a cake.

KENNEDY. I ain't never tasted no black pussy before.

JUNE *slams down the receiver.*

GLORIA. Now, what you do that for? Poor boy pluck up the courage to call.

KENNEDY *turns up the sound on the television.*

He is watching a news report of the race riots on the television.

We hear the sound of sirens and burning buildings.

KENNEDY *remains onstage.*

He is alone in his bedroom but he is placed between the TWINS *onstage.*

He watches the news footage of the riots whilst drinking and masturbating.

During the above, the TWINS *have brought typewriters out from under the bed.*

They pound the keys.

They speak in American accents.

JENNIFER. 'He pulled me into his arms and we danced like mad for a moment.'

JUNE. 'His eyes slipped down to her cloche-shaped breast. He was aware of a concupiscence running through his mind.'

JENNIFER. 'The music changed and we watched as everyone became hysterical. There were teenagers all around jumping on each other, pulling anybody to the floor with salacious frenzy.'

JUNE. 'There was a brief, constrained silence. She stared down at her wedding ring, twisting it. She laughed and tossed her hair back strenuously.'

JENNIFER. 'They screamed loudly to the music, pulling out blades and stabbing their best friend to death. Police sirens and shrieking ambulance bells filled my ears.'

Both TWINS *ferociously pound their typewriters.*

KENNEDY *removes his shirt and wipes the sweat from his body.*

GLORIA, *in her dressing gown, bangs on the door.*

KENNEDY *exits.*

GLORIA. It's the middle of the night. This is the third time this week.

The TWINS *gather the pages of their novels.*

And me up first thing in the morning to look after little Philip while Greta take the baby for her vaccination. I only hope the kitchen don't stay the same way you left it last night. Cocoa spilt on the floor. Chocolate fingerprints all over the fridge door. Go to sleep, you hear.

The TWINS *are gathering the pages from the floor and each stuffing them into an A4 envelope.*

JUNE *reads the letter they are putting into the envelope.*

JUNE. 'Please find enclosed our novels, *Pepsi Cola Addict.*'

JENNIFER. 'And *Discomania.*'

JUNE is addressing the envelope as JENNIFER *feeds the address.*

JENNIFER. New Horizon.

Self Publishing.

54 Acacia Avenue.

Bognor Regis.

Sussex.

JENNIFER *unlocks the door and pushes the envelope into* GLORIA*'s hands.*

GLORIA. When I knock this door in four hours you'd best be up, dressed, and ready to sign on.

And from it – you a go pay me the mountain a postage you swindle from me to fund your nonsense. Go to sleep.

JENNIFER *locks the door.*

JUNE *is reading their horoscope in* Jackie *magazine.*

JUNE. Look, Jen, it's written in our stars.

(*Reading from* Jackie *magazine*.) 'The moon moves into Saturn and triggers an exciting week for Aries for any new venture or long-cherished dream. There could be an interesting telephone call or letter on Friday. Lady Diana is not the only one to go to the ball next week.'

Lights change.

Binoculars

From their treasure trove under the bed, JUNE *pulls out some binoculars.*

We hear the sound of the television.

It is the morning of the Royal Wedding between Charles and Diana.

GLORIA *is drying a plate with a Royal Wedding tea towel while watching the BBC coverage.*

The reporter is referring to the suspense over Lady Diana's wedding dress.

GLORIA. Greta say she have three-quarter-length sleeve but I think longer. Me think pearl for buttons on the cuff. Ten, maybe twelve pearl button on the cuff. Ah well, we'll know soon enough. Rosie, get out the way of the screen. We no need no street party. We a go have our own party indoors.

Upstairs, the TWINS *are looking out of an imaginary window facing the audience.*

We can hear the muffled sound of the Royal Wedding commentary from the television below.

JUNE *peers through the binoculars.*

JUNE. His curtains are still closed.

JENNIFER. Maybe he's gone out.

(*Looking at her watch.*) It's my turn now.

JUNE (*still looking through the binoculars*). They've finished the bunting. They're putting out the tables.

JENNIFER. Five minutes each.

JUNE. Woman from number 23 had her hair cut like Lady Di. (*Suddenly excited.*) I can see him!

JENNIFER. Where?

JENNIFER *looks frantically through the window.*

JUNE. Downstairs. He's wearing his new baseball cap. The red one with the star. The one he wore last Sunday.

JENNIFER. Give me the binoculars. (*Grabs the binoculars.*)

JUNE. He's gone.

JENNIFER. You didn't see him.

JUNE. I did.

GLORIA *knocks at the door.*

GLORIA. Letter come for you. Hurry up and take. Me a miss the commentary.

JENNIFER *goes to the door and unlocks it.*

(*Handing* JUNE *the letter.*) You should see the street of London. Look like the whole world come to see the Princess on her wedding day. You come down later see the dress?

JUNE *closes and locks the door. She reads the words on the letter.*

JUNE (*excited*). 'New Horizons.'

JENNIFER. Let me see.

JUNE. Addressed to me.

JUNE *opens the letter and reads.*

'We are delighted to inform you that we are interested in publishing your novel.'

JENNIFER *grabs the letter and reads it, wild with disappointment and envy.*

49

JENNIFER. Where's a tramp like you gonna get nine hundred and eighty pounds?

JENNIFER goes to her bunk bed and climbs under the duvet.

She puts her head under the pillow.

JUNE climbs the bed frame to try to console her.

JUNE. Maybe your letter will come tomorrow.

JENNIFER. I don't want a letter.

JUNE tries to cling onto the frame but JENNIFER forces her to let go.

JUNE. We can get the money.

JENNIFER. Leave me alone.

JUNE. We'll find a way.

JENNIFER. Get away from me.

JENNIFER pushes JUNE to the floor.

JUNE (*suddenly*). Cathy would lend us the money.

Beat.

I'm gonna ring her.

I'm gonna ask her.

I'm going to ring Cathy from the phone box.

JUNE pulls a suitcase out from under the bed.

She pulls out armfuls of clothes.

She finds a pair of jeans and a parka and dresses herself, taking off her skirt.

She pulls the hood up over her head and puts on sunglasses.

She goes to the door.

She turns the key in the lock.

JENNIFER realises JUNE is actually going to leave her.

She leaps from the bed and slams the door shut.

JENNIFER *pulls on jeans and a parka.*

As JENNIFER *dresses,* GLORIA *is watching Lady Diana come out in her wedding dress.*

She calls up to JUNE *and* JENNIFER.

GLORIA. Quick, she's coming down the steps of the golden carriage. Quick, quick, you have to see the dress, all big and white and beautiful. Catches her waist like so, and billow, billows to the ground and forty yards behind. And the horses all pert and white, standing to attention.

We hear the sound of the crowds cheering as Lady Diana emerges in her wedding dress.

GLORIA*'s face lights up as she sees the* TWINS *coming downstairs.*

Him like a prince out of a fairy story. Come and see, she look perfect.

GLORIA *watches as the* TWINS *go out through the front door.*

Where are you going?

(*Shouting after them.*) Tonight of all nights –

The front door slams.

– you choose to venture when the Princess she just married.

And what in God's name are you wearing?

Lights change.

KENNEDY *enters with a ghetto blaster playing heavy metal at top volume.*

He throws the mattresses from JUNE *and* JENNIFER*'s bed to the ground.*

He scatters a bin bag of his belongings all over them, to create his room.

He lies on his bed, reading.

Lights change.

The TWINS *step out onto the street.*

We hear the sound of the Royal Wedding street party.

JUNE. Don't look at anyone.

JENNIFER *looks through the binoculars.*

They squeeze into the phone box on the corner.

JUNE *presses the buttons on the phone.*

CATHY, *at home, is carrying a phone and a child's toy.*

CATHY. Hello.

JUNE (*whispers*). She's answered.

CATHY. Cathy speaking. Hello.

JUNE *listens for a few moments and then slams the phone down.*

JENNIFER, *still peering through the binoculars, screams.*

JENNIFER. It's him. (*Whispers.*) He's leaving the house. He's closing the door. Crossing the street. He's coming this way.

The phone rings back.

JUNE *picks it up.*

CATHY. Did you ring this number?

JENNIFER (*whispers*). It's him. It's him.

Coming this way.

CATHY. Hello.

Is there anybody there?

Hello.

Speak to me.

Hello.

I know you're there.

Hello.

Can you please tell me who this is?

It's all right, darling.

It's all right, sweetheart. Mummy's here.

JUNE *drops the receiver.*

The phone goes dead.

JENNIFER. You've just missed him. (*She looks through the binoculars again.*) The curtains are closed. Car's gone. No one's home.

JUNE. Let's break in.

SMASH. The TWINS *break a window in the back of* KENNEDY*'s house.*

They clamber in through the window.

Watch the broken glass.

It is pitch black in the house with its curtains closed.

JENNIFER. What's he gonna do when he gets back?

JUNE. What are we gonna do is a better question.

JENNIFER. There's his cap. And his shirt. Smell it.

JUNE. His camera.

JUNE *picks up a camera and takes a photo of* KENNEDY*'s shirt, which causes a flash in the dark.*

JUNE *takes a flash photo of* JENNIFER *smelling the shirt.*

JENNIFER. Here's his pants.

JUNE *takes photo.*

JENNIFER *puts them in her pocket.*

Lie on his bed.

JUNE. I dare you.

JENNIFER *climbs on* KENNEDY*'s bed.*

JUNE *takes flash photo.*

The front door downstairs slams.

The TWINS *freeze.*

KENNEDY *is coming up the stairs*.

KENNEDY. I've got a fucking baseball bat.

JENNIFER (*whispers*). He hasn't, it's here.

KENNEDY *runs in, waving his bottle of vodka like a baseball bat*.

JUNE *takes a flash photo of* KENNEDY.

KENNEDY. You could have just knocked on the fucking door, you've caused a helluva fucking draught.

KENNEDY *snatches the binoculars off* JENNIFER.

He peers out the window at the Royal Wedding street party.

We can hear the DJ announcing the next dance.

Look at 'em. Bunch of fucking sheep. No wasps. No fucking honey bees.

Gathering, gathering, gathering. Just pumping into the system. Just squeezing into the hive to feed the Queen bee, Lady Di, who kept her pussy clean because she knew its fucking value.

KENNEDY *forces* JENNIFER *to look through the binoculars*.

Look at 'em.

KENNEDY *forces* JUNE.

JENNIFER *takes pictures of* KENNEDY, *the street*, JUNE, *the room, as* KENNEDY *speaks*.

Out till all hours with their stupid fucking tablecloths. And their stupid fucking 'bunting'. This is bread and circuses. Do you really think old Charlie boy would be marrying if it wasn't for the riots? They've read their Roman history well. That fucking charade is to calm the masses. Look at them. They really fucking think they're involved. They really think they're at the wedding party. It's the same as the days of squires, hey. No fucking change there. Just the fiefdoms are bigger. You live in one big fiefdom. Did you know that? Still working your ass to the bone to put lamb on their table. And you sniff the bone.

That's if you're lucky. We should cut the fucking lot down. Every last little red, white and blue flag, and burn it. You been watching the news lately? All those brave knaves in the fucking riots, your people, man, in the name of all peasants, and a shithole like this is raising the flag to their own fucking oppressor. This fucking island makes me fucking laugh.

Anyhow. Fuck that. Did you like my little shows? I knew you were watching me. I bet you had a wank. Do you wank together or do you wank separately?

Back to back. That'd be good. That'd look really fucking good. Like an Athena poster. Naked. Back to back. That's a real good picture. Take your coats off. I said, take your coats off and sit down. Back to back.

KENNEDY *forces the* TWINS *to sit down.*

Back to back, I said.

In unison, the TWINS *swivel on their bums to sit back to back.*

That's it. Now put a hand to your head. Like you're using an afro comb. Your other hand.

In unison, the TWINS *put their left hands to their heads.*

Now one between your legs. Between your legs. Rabbits, the legs.

KENNEDY *grabs both* TWINS' *arms and forces them to put their right hands between their legs.*

He finds his camera.

Told yer. A fucking photo shoot.

KENNEDY *takes the flash photo.*

You need to take your tops off. Show your bras. Like a bikini top. Like you're sat on sand. Like it's exotic.

Through the corner of their eyes, the TWINS *try to see each other.*

Don't turn around.

KENNEDY *shouts out of the window at the street party.*

Turn that shit off.

KENNEDY *punches the cassette button on.*

Heavy metal.

Take your top off.

Neither TWIN *responds, they just stay in the position he has put them in.*

KENNEDY *is building a spliff.*

KENNEDY *parodies the Myers-Briggs psychological test used earlier by* CATHY *at Eastgate.*

Okay. So now we're all comfortable, I'm going to find out some more about Jennifer and June. I know that you wank when your mum and dad are asleep. I know that you have two sisters and a brother. I've brought with me some substances to help you relax while you answer my questions.

KENNEDY *names the substance as he places them on the floor beside the* TWINS.

Weed.

Glue.

And Vodka.

KENNEDY *starts to roll the joint.*

I've bought with me some boxes.

This box – (*Pointing at himself.*) is called Mr Somebody: me, Kennedy.

I'm going to put him over here on his own.

I'm going to ask you questions.

You point to the box to show me your answer.

You don't have to speak.

Unless you want to.

Are you sure you don't want to take your shirts off?

Neither TWIN *replies or moves.*

KENNEDY *finishes rolling his joint.*

Who will make you laugh?

The TWINS *eye the joint and shyly titter.*

(*Smiling at the spliff.*) You're right. You're dead right.

KENNEDY *takes a drag and then hands it to* JENNIFER, *who takes a drag.*

Don't pull in too far on your first go. Just breathe easy. Take it slowly. That's right. You're a natural.

KENNEDY *picks up the glue.*

So who will comfort you when you are sad?

JUNE *reaches towards the glue.*

Good choice. Very good choice. Put the bag around your face like so.

Breathe in. Don't panic when you feel the first sensation. You have to ride with it. Okay.

JUNE *breathes in the glue.*

What will loosen your fucking tongue?

KENNEDY *doesn't wait for a reply but fills a glass with vodka.*

Both TWINS *try to eye each other out of the corner of their eyes.*

JENNIFER *grabs the glass and drinks the vodka in one shot.*

KENNEDY *whoops, punching the air.*

Who understands you the best?

In unison, they point at KENNEDY.

And it's Mr Somebody who knows your dirty little secret.

Still standing over them, KENNEDY *pulls at the* TWINS' *jumpers.*

Lift your arms so they slide over your head.

Come on, you've had enough poses out of me.

The TWINS *take off their tops.*

They are no longer in unison but in competition in their desire to please KENNEDY.

KENNEDY *steps back and takes more pictures now they have no top on.*

Eenny, meany, miny, moe, catch a nigger by its toe.

KENNEDY *grabs* JUNE*'s feet.*

JUNE *screams and clings to* JENNIFER.

When it squeal let it go.

KENNEDY *lets* JUNE *go.*

And grabs JENNIFER*'s feet.*

KENNEDY *drags* JENNIFER *to make her lie down.*

JENNIFER *suddenly grabs hold of* KENNEDY *and tries to kiss him.*

At this moment, GLORIA *enters.*

She is at home, watching television.

The BBC Royal Wedding commentary continues in the background.

GLORIA. Here she come! Here she come! Out onto the balcony of Buckingham Palace! Oh my goodness. Can't believe it all happen so soon. Seem like only five minutes ago she get engaged and now she the future Queen of Hingland. What a difference a day make, eh, Rosie? What a difference.

While GLORIA *speaks,* KENNEDY *climbs on top of* JENNIFER *and shags her.*

JUNE *watches, paralysed with rage and jealousy.*

KENNEDY *cums and climbs off.*

The TWINS *fight.*

KENNEDY, *buttoning up his pants, grabs the camera.*

He takes photographs as the girls grapple at each other's throats.

We hear 'Land of Hope and Glory' playing outside.

As JUNE *forces* JENNIFER *to the ground,* KENNEDY *mounts* JUNE *from behind.*

Throughout, JUNE *keeps hold of* JENNIFER*'s hair and they look into each other's eyes.*

(*Clapping her hands with excitement.*) Oh my goodness. Him kiss her! Him kiss her! Look at the crowd gone wild!

We hear the crowds cheering and the Royal Wedding commentary as Charles kisses Diana on the balcony of Buckingham Palace.

KENNEDY *rolls off* JUNE.

Lights change.

KENNEDY *gets a sausage roll.*

He picks up the binoculars and goes straight to the window.

The TWINS *watch every mouthful he eats.*

He is watching the Royal Wedding street party.

KENNEDY. You see, that was the fucking point of school. All that moral shit to block the nourishment of our own fucking thoughts. They train the stupid ones to be good. And the intelligent ones like me and you they label: non-worker bee – and keep them away from the hive at all cost.

Thank God I'm leaving this fucking island in the morning.

The TWINS *both stare at* KENNEDY.

Didn't you know? Daddy's been posted back home. Back to the 'Land of the Free'.

Lights change.

It is the following morning.

Daylight.

The TWINS *enter the bedroom.*

The TWINS *carry on looking out of the window at the sky.*

They are both distraught.

JUNE. He'll be getting on his plane.

JUNE starts to cry.

JENNIFER *tries to stifle her sobs.*

A strange, desperate struggle ensues as JENNIFER *tries to stop* JUNE *crying.*

They are each trying to comfort and stifle the other.

JENNIFER, *inconsolable, whispers into* JUNE*'s ear as* GLORIA *speaks.*

GLORIA (*knocking on the door. Trying to force the lock*). Where you two been all night? You open this door. What you think you playing at? Me and your daddy up half the night worrying. Little Rosie crying. Why you have to spoil it? Spoil our special day. You open this door right now and tell me where you been.

JENNIFER, *crying, whispers into* JUNE*'s ear.*

JENNIFER. You are Jennifer. You are Jennifer. You are me.

GLORIA (*from the other side of the door*). This weekend you coming with me to the Sunday School. Monday we go sign you onto City and Guilds' secretarial course. Put your typing to some use for a change. We'll have no more of your foolish schemes and fancies. No more writing in the middle of the night like you possessed. Youwedd learn to live in the real world like the rest of us. You hear? Do you hear me? You learn to do as you told. Do you hear what I'm telling you?

As GLORIA *speaks, the lights darken.*

The TWINS *begin to pull everything out from under their bed.*

Dolls and paraphernalia, Christmas tree, cassette recorder, piles of writing, The Writing School and The Art of Conversation *manuals, even the uniforms they wore.*

They pile them up in the middle of their room.

From the pile, JUNE *retrieves an old* Jackie *magazine.*

JENNIFER *picks up a Barbie.*

They light the Jackie *magazine and use it to set fire to the Barbie's dress and hair.*

They toss them onto the pyre as JUNE *throws vodka onto the flames.*

The fire kindles and grows until it is a massive blaze.

Amidst the sound of sirens, the TWINS *ring the police from the phone box.*

They tell them in clear speech:

JUNE *and* JENNIFER. We've burned down Sir Thomas Picton Secondary Modern.

The End.

A Nick Hern Book

Speechless, based on the book *The Silent Twins* by Marjorie Wallace, first published in Great Britain in 2010 as a paperback original by Nick Hern Books Limited, 14 Larden Road, London W3 7ST, in association with Shared Experience and Sherman Cymru

Speechless copyright © 2010 Linda Brogan and Polly Teale
The Silent Twins by Marjorie Wallace first published in Great Britain in 1986

Linda Brogan and Polly Teale have asserted their moral right to be identified as the authors of this work

Front cover photo by Barnaby Hall / Getty Images and Eureka! Design Consultants Ltd
Cover design by Ned Hoste, 2H

Typeset by Nick Hern Books, London
Printed in the UK by CPI Bookmarque, Croydon, Surrey

A CIP catalogue record for this book is available from the British Library

ISBN 978 1 84842 128 8

Mixed Sources
Product group from well-managed forests and other controlled sources
www.fsc.org   Cert no. TT-COC-002227
© 1996 Forest Stewardship Council